THE RUGGED ROADTRIP

Darren Brett Conrad

THE RUGGED ROADTRIP

Darren Brett Conrad

PRINTED IN THE UNITED STATES OF AMERICA

ISBN: 9798887572116

DISCLAIMER: This book is my personal history and thereby relates stories that have happened during my own lifetime and from my own perspective. Many of the names of persons mentioned in this book have been changed to protect their identities. Others, whose actual names I have used, have agreed to be written about in this book in the manner described. This book has been written for educational and entertainment purposes only, and it cannot guarantee that the reader will be able to successfully start, own, and/or run a business or achieve success regarding any other topic as discussed within these pages.

Book cover design: Doug Paul, DPaul Art

Interior design: Deborah Perdue, Illumination Graphics

Dedication with a Message of Hope

To those who are struggling with alcohol, addiction, loss of a loved one, loneliness, or financial insecurity and are looking for God and seeking a relationship with Him . . .

To those who have been ignited with the entrepreneurial spirit and who wish to serve others . . .

I pray that my story, this lifelong journey upon which God has guided me, inspires you to write and share your own story . . .

"Ask, and it shall be given you;

seek, and ye shall find;

knock, and it shall be opened unto you."

Matthew 7:7

Acknowledgements

To the Lord our God on High, I give YOU the glory and the honor. I do not want to take any credit for the writing of this story without stating that He gave it all for me to do. This book was inspired by God, and everything He has given me, from my parents to my siblings, to the people whom He has put in my path. He is Alpha and He is Omega, the beginning and the end. And still what is yet to come.

To my family, who have always been supportive of me,

My mom and stepdad, Jennifer and John Boutselis,

My father, Steve Conrad,

My sister, Noelle Gilson,

My brothers John and Dan Boutselis, and my sister-in-law,
Carley Boutselis

To my friends and all of the people that God has placed in my path, His messengers, His teachers, His mentors,

Jerry Williams

Scott and Daphene Andrew

Valter Amaral

Mike Bella

David Harmer

Brad Loy

George Varn

John Grof

Amy Bowen

Gary Davis

Kyle Sherratt

Steve Jones

Jay Murphy

Lucy Kucerova

Aaron Wales

These are just a few. There are many more. Thank you!

Introduction

I have never been one to keep a diary about the events of my life. Instead, I keep a photo journal that I scroll through, every now and then, to remember faces, places, and events.

These photos, however, are more than just memories. They are like a collage, emphasizing the high points my life, including the amazing people I have known and the amazing places that I have visited. While some of those friendships and relationships have remained strong, others have ended, I still choose to see the good in each and every one of them.

"Connect the dots backwards," Steve Jobs once said. As I reflect upon my life, I recognize that each happening or event in my life has acted as a steppingstone to the past. For in my past there were times when circumstances did not look promising, but I always maintained my faith and trusted that things would improve. To some, this may sound cliché, but I can say, in reflecting upon the past 50 years of my life, that this story rings true. My life did not happen according to my original plans. In fact, my life has unfolded in ways, some strange and some wonderful, much better than I could have ever imagined.

If I had to summarize who I am in once sentence, I would say that I am a simple man who has lived a complex life. Like many people, my life has had its share of struggles and obstacles, yet it has also been filled with blessings and much joy and happiness.

When I was six years old, my parents divorced, and I became the man of the house. I lived with my mother and my older sister in an affluent suburb of Columbus, Ohio. I attended school and spent summers thousands of miles away at my dad's house, either in Berlin, Germany, Fairfax, Virginia, or wherever Dad was stationed with the U.S. Army. Being away for the entire summer made it hard for me to maintain the friendships I had made during the school year. I started drinking when I was 12 years old as a way to connect with my peers. In hindsight, this was an unhealthy way to make friends, but it worked. I continued drinking throughout my adolescent years into mid-life. Even though others recognized that I had a drinking problem, I never saw myself as an alcoholic, at least not until I got into trouble.

During my pre-teen years, my mom got remarried. This might seem like an awkward situation for a kid, but I liked my stepdad, John, whom I also call "Pops." He is a smart and wise man who started and ran a successful family business, Boutselis Auto Care, in Columbus, Ohio. Like him, I had an entrepreneurial spirit, but I also had a wild side that I could not control. I dropped out of high school at age 15 and ran away from home for a couple of weeks which did not go over well with my mother. She kicked me out of the house and I moved to Arizona to live with my dad. Little did I know that in Arizona I was about to experience one of the biggest obstacles in my young adult life.

One afternoon, when I was jogging on the side of the road, I was hit by a cyclist. I suffered a severe head injury and was life flighted to a hospital where I underwent neurosurgery. When I woke up from the operation, the doctor told me that I would never play sports again or be able to concentrate on my studies. Instead of feeling sad or angry about the grim prognosis, I looked at it as a challenge. I started studying more and improved my grades. I started walking, then running, then playing sports again.

Throughout this time, I never gave up alcohol, however. My dad, being the no-nonsense man that he was, shipped me back to Ohio when he caught me having a party at the house. Ironically, I re-enrolled in my old high school in Ohio, the one I had dropped out of. I was not what one would consider a good student, but I attended classes with kids much younger than me and graduated at age 19.

For the next five years I became a successful businessman, at first by selling Cutco knives, then by opening up my own office and managing salespeople. But something was missing from that picture of success. I did not have a college degree. I applied to Ohio State University, and, at age 24, was accepted. I eventually joined a fraternity, which did not help my drinking problem, although it helped me hone my business skills. My plan after college was to work in the pharmaceutical field but my life did not go according to my plans. Instead, I started working in the mattress industry. I enjoyed the challenge of building the business. For me, it was less about selling mattresses and more about helping customers receive superior products at a great value. That mindset has helped me create and develop a dynamic business model over the years that has helped entrepreneurs in the industry achieve amazing success.

Since then, I have started, owned, and operated four multi-million-dollar businesses, but I have also been sued which resulted in the loss of those businesses. At the time I was running those businesses, I was still heavily drinking to the point of getting kicked off of an airplane, out of a football game, and off of a cruise. In 2008, I decided to stop drinking, which dramatically changed my life for the better.

If there is one common thread in all of the obstacles I have faced—whether during my alcoholic or sober years, whether starting businesses or losing businesses, whether when I was getting married or getting divorced—it was my perseverance and desire to move forward no matter how bad things appeared to be. I always had faith that things would work out in the long run. Eventually, this faith grew to the point where I recognized my place in the divine scheme of things, which has changed my life in so many ways.

Even in our darkest hours, when we think all is lost, something better always comes along. I could look at every obstacle that has occurred in my life, or at least what I believed to be an obstacle, and realize that it was not an obstacle at all, just a change in my life's trajectory.

When I "connect my own dots backwards," I realize that my life has been one heck of a rugged road trip. My story is the story of an underdog who has had to overcome numerous challenges against all odds. My story is also a story of surrender. A surrender to alcohol, a surrender to my business plans, and a surrender to what I thought was good for me in my personal relationships.

Within these pages, I invite you to come along with me on this rugged road trip, to experience its twists and turns, its upward climbs and downward spirals, its thrills and its less-than-stellar moments, so that you can also apply these experiences to your own life wherever you are right now.

Everyone's life is a journey. No one has the same path. Life is more about how you respond to your journey and accept it for what it is. When you consider your challenges as gifts, as well as the experiences that are a result of those challenges, you will learn to stop fighting and ultimately surrender!

So, are you ready to embark on a journey? If you are, I invite you to put on your seatbelt, kick back, and go for a ride. Let's experience this rugged road trip called life together!

– Darren Conrad

Timeline

1985	Began attending Upper Arlington High School in Ohio as a freshman.
1986	Dropped out of Upper Arlington H.S. Moved to Arizona to live with my dad, Steve Conrad.
1986-1988	Attended Buena High School in Arizona.
Aug. 29, 1987	Suffered a head injury while road running. Underwent extensive neurosurgery.
1989	Returned to Ohio to live with Mom and Pops, Jennifer and John Boutselis. Graduated from Upper Arlington H.S. at age 19.
1989-1994	Began working for Vector Marketing selling Cutco Knives. Promoted to District Manager.
1995-1998	Attended and graduated from The Ohio State University (OSU) in Columbus, Ohio.
1999-2000	Worked for CollegeClub.com upon graduating from OSU.
2000-2003	Did contract work for previous friend's (Jack's) company, Power Marketing Direct (PMD).
Nov. 2, 2001	Married my first wife, Melanie; Divorced in 2005.
2003-2009	Moved To South Carolina. Created, owned, and operated Carolina Bedding.
Feb. 2004	Sued by Jack for alleged non-compete agreement violation with PMD.

Nov. 22, 2008	Achieved sobriety.
April 1, 2009	Received judgement from PMD lawsuit.
2011-2012	Created, owned, and operated Carolina Bedding Direct.
July 14, 2012	My younger brother Daniel Boutselis passed away.
2013	Created, owned, and operated Mattress by Appointment (MBA).
May 4, 2013	Married 2nd wife Chloe; Divorced 2016.
2015-2016	Created, owned, and operated Mattress Direct after being served with lawsuit from previous business partner with MBA.
May 15, 2015	Left Florida, drove cross country, and moved to California after receiving judgement from MBA lawsuit.
2016-2017	Unofficially helped grow RSS/BoxDrop with business processes, recruitment, and training programs.
March 2017	Returned to Florida after global settlement on ALL lawsuits.
2017-Present	Began working with RSS/Box Drop® in an official capacity and as part-owner.
2019	Drove cross-country on my 1st Rugged Road Trip for RSS/Box Drop®.
Aug.5, 2019	Married my 3rd wife Grace; Divorced 2020.

2020	Drove cross-country on my 2nd official Rugged Road Trip for RSS/Box Drop®.
2021	Drove cross-country on my 3rd official Rugged Road Trip for RSS/Box Drop®.
Dec. 31, 2021	Younger brother John Boutselis Jr. married Carley Berarducci in Columbus, Ohio.
2022	Drove cross-country on my 4th Rugged Road Trip for RSS/BoxDrop®.

PART I

The Surrendering

Chapter One

I had been helping my good friend Dallas Mills unload a truckload of headboards into his Jacksonville mattress store when my cell phone started buzzing in my back pocket. It was one of those muggy summer nights. No stars. No breeze. Just thick and humid air. I pulled my phone out of my pocket and looked at the screen. The sky was pitch black, my cell phone the only visible light. I immediately recognized the number. "Can you hold up a minute, Nighthawk?" I asked Dallas. "I need to take this call."

Dallas nodded with understanding. "Sure. Go ahead, Dragon. No problem."

It was my attorney calling.

My ex-business partner with Mattress By Appointment (MBA) had filed a lawsuit against me personally as well as against my current company, Mattress Direct. The legal complaint read that I had breached a dealer territory agreement with MBA. I, however, had never signed such an agreement because I had never worked for MBA as a dealer. I was, in fact, the sole creator and owner of MBA. It was now a tricky situation, however. My ex-partner, with whom I had entered into a business relationship later on, still owned 45 percent of the shares. It is a long story, but let's just say for now that he was able to take full ownership of MBA in what I would call a sly game of business chess. Now that I was no longer a partner of MBA, my attorneys informed me that I was legally free and clear to start a new company. I did and called it Mattress Direct. But now I was being sued for starting it.

When I created Mattress Direct, some of the best leadership left MBA to follow me. Kyle Sherratt, a good, family man, became my general manager. Troy Meath, who had a magical way of connecting with people, became my national recruiter. We formed a powerful, unstoppable team. Together, we were like the Three Musketeers, the final three strikes in the 10th frame of a bowling game, the perfect geometrical golden triangle. A good number of MBA dealers also left and joined Mattress Direct. They knew that my previous partner had been fired by MBA's Board of Directors for spreading lies about me. They also knew that he took the company away from me when I was financially and emotionally vulnerable.

I had formed genuine relationships with the dealers, people whom I genuinely cared about, people whom I wanted to see succeed as entrepreneurs. Within seven months, my new company, Mattress Direct, had dealers in 50 locations throughout the country. Our company culture and mindset of valuing our dealers, valuing our customers, and believing in our products ignited the business to spread like wildfire.

"Darren here," I said as I took the call from my attorney. I was expecting good news.

After the preliminary injunction hearing three months ago, I felt as if I had a solid defense and a good legal representation in C.F., a local Jacksonville Beach attorney. The three-day hearing that took place in the judge's chambers seemed as if it was headed in a positive direction for me as well. With my previous partner and his attorneys sitting opposite me and my attorneys, and the judge and his court reporter sitting at the head of the table, we spent three days listening to in-person and live video depositions from witnesses whose testimony was in my favor. After the hearing, the court reporter even asked me for my telephone number for her husband who was interested in starting a business. After the hearing was over, the judge joked with me in the parking lot that I had nothing to worry about. My attorney also expressed his opinion that the case would end in my favor.

"Hey, Darren," my attorney answered. He was speaking so quickly that I couldn't have interrupted him if I tried. I listened, but I didn't like the bits and pieces of what I was hearing.

"But I don't work in a store anyway," I interjected. "Can't I keep doing what I do on the phone?"

"Would you be doing that within the 30-mile radius?" he asked tersely, without emotion.

"Well…technically…yes, if I work from home." I now lived in Jacksonville Beach, Florida, and that would definitely fall within the "no-business" zone ordered by the injunction that my attorney was telling me I now had to follow. Helping out at Dallas's store would also be a no-go.

"Then, you can't do business," he said matter-of-factly.

The conversation left me speechless. I couldn't believe the news. I was devastated.

I put my phone back into my pocket and looked at Dallas. "The store's officially yours," I said, still in disbelief. "Looks like I'm out of business."

"What?" Dallas said, looking as surprised as I felt. After leaving the police force, he had been looking for a business opportunity. He had never run a business. He had never sold mattresses. So, I helped him set up the showroom, and he let me to use it as a place to meet and interview potential Mattress Direct dealers.

Dallas's store was located in a business strip mall. The location was small in comparison to typical mattress storefronts. It was about 1,500-square feet and offered a line-up of nine select mattresses. It was not open to the public; instead, customers were invited by appointment for a private consultation. This business model that I had created was simple and unique. The showroom could also be easily duplicated at any location in the country.

"Look, don't worry, Dallas. I'll give you everything," I said. "I'll give you the direct contacts to the mattress manufacturer, too." My main concern was not for myself. It was about keeping my commitment to the dealers who needed support. These were families who were paying their rent or mortgages. Families who needed to put food on the table.

While my attorney advised that I could still run Mattress Direct, any business dealings would need to be conducted outside of the 30-mile radius. That was like telling me I could play the game, but I would have to duct tape my feet together and have my hands tied behind my back. Legally, I could no longer use Dallas's store showroom to recruit new dealers, and I could not help Dallas nor the 49 other dealers run their businesses from my home. It was a dilemma because, morally, I could not leave these good people out in the cold to fend for themselves

How did I get into the mattress industry? I had never dreamed

I would. For the most part, it is a tough industry to break into because it is mainly run by family-owned businesses. In 2000, a friend and fraternity brother from Ohio State University named Jack had started a company called Power Marketing Direct (PMD) in Columbus, Ohio. Jack's invitation to work with PMD as a 1099 contractor was attractive because I was looking for a new opportunity.

One of the things I did was design a simple business model that helped people unfamiliar with the industry start and run a successful mattress business. I also served as a national trainer and recruiter for the company. Things were going well. The business was growing. But, after three years, I was ready for a change because I no longer believed in PMD's mission. When I informed Jack that I was leaving the company and needed my final paycheck, he would not give it to me until I signed a noncompete agreement. I did not want to sign because I had always worked for him as a 1099 contractor. I had witnesses to this coercion and felt I would be legally covered if others saw me being forced to sign the against my will. My main focus at the time was getting my paycheck. I signed on the dotted line and forgot about it. A few months later, my wife and I sold our home in Columbus, Ohio, and moved with her children to South Carolina, where we bought a beautiful home. As soon as we got settled in, I started my own company, Carolina Bedding. I did not even have to recruit dealers. Within the first year, I already had 50 dealers, most based upon referrals.

Things were going well for us. Six months later, Jack found out that I had started my own company. He filed a lawsuit against me. My stomach was in knots. I had never been sued before and did not know what to expect. The complaint stated that I had breached a dealer and territory agreement. To my surprise, Jack took me to court, and he won. I was ordered to pay a judgement, as well as PMD's attorney's and legal fees, which totaled $650,000. The lawsuit left me in great debt and was a financial drain on my assets. But I was determined to work through the challenges and prevail.

Ten years later, in 2013, in a "what goes around comes around" or "karma" situation, a man named Scott Andrew, a previous dealer for PMD and now owner of Retail Service Systems, Inc. (RSS), filed and won a lawsuit against PMD. In the judgement, he was awarded PMD's intellectual property secrets. Jack lost PMD and the judgement against me was now in the hands of RSS which continued to drain my bank accounts.

Originally, my plan had been to build up Mattress Direct then later merge with PMD. I wanted to be the big fish. But I had been pulled from the sea still pierced with a hook in my mouth. RSS caught me whole and swallowed me up in a big fish-little fish scenario. I no longer had any leverage and was totally defenseless.

Getting back to the story at hand, I was not about to abandon my Mattress Direct dealers who had been loyal to me. I was not sure at first how I could help them. I certainly was not going to suggest that they work with my ex-partner at MBA. There was only one person I could think of that might be able to help, the same person who was currently suing me due to the acquisition of my judgement from PMD, Scott Andrew, the CEO of RSS. Scott was not a bad person for trying to collect on the judgement. Technically, that was just a legality. It was nothing personal. A few years prior, I had met Scott informally and found him to be quite amicable. The issue was not about judgements or personalities. The question was if my dealers would be happy under RSS leadership. There was only one way for me to find out.

I pulled out my cell phone and looked for Scott in my contacts list. He was still there.

As I dialed his number, I thought about how my life always has a way of coming around full circle. Here I was calling a man who was suing me in order to help my MD dealers. The whole idea of asking Scott to help seemed strange and impractical, even to me. I was not sure what Scott would say, but this was the only option I could think of at the time.

"Hey Scott," I said as he picked up the phone. "I'm out. I just received an order."

We spoke a short while, mainly me explaining to him that the Mattress Direct dealers needed service and support, and that part of me also did not want to lose what I had built with the company. I needed to come up with a strategy that was both moral and legal. I knew that I could not sell Scott my dealer contracts because I did not have contracts with the Mattress Direct dealers. Due to all of the previous litigation I had experienced over the years, I was anti-contract. I truly believed that if I provided excellent service and support to the dealers that it would be enough for them to want to work with me and that had proven true.

As Scott and I continued the conversation, we soon both realized that the solution to this dilemma would have to take into consideration that my ex- partner was also in litigation with him, just in separate lawsuits. My previous partner was suing me, and Scott was suing him. It was a complex situation. We knew that the solution would have to be creative. Scott and I agreed on the first step, which was to connect him with Kyle and Troy, my current business partners. It was my hope that at least the Mattress Direct leadership and some of the dealers would join RSS, and the business could continue to thrive and grow. This was never about me. It was about the people and the business I had created. I just could not let things go.

We ended the call and I felt shaky. I knew that my hand had been played. I would just have to wait and see if my business partners and the dealers would follow suit.

Chapter Two

After Mattress Direct's first incentive trip in the fall of 2014, I realized my marriage to Chloe, a beautiful woman with long blonde hair, a nice smile, and a slim physique, was facing some challenges. This was also the second marriage for both of us. We had only been married a little more than a year when I found myself facing the loss of the company I had built, Mattress By Appointment or MBA.

Now I was losing another company, Mattress Direct. Before the filing of the lawsuit from my ex-partner, Mattress Direct held its first incentive trip in Mexico. It was much smaller than the trips I had attended in previous years with previous companies which I had either owned and operated or worked for. I considered this smaller number of attendees to be a blessing because it made our gathering all the more intimate. My Mattress Direct business partners and their families travelled in our group, as well as some of the previous MBA dealers and their families who had followed us to Mattress Direct.

The trip was held at the Hotel Riu Palace Riviera Maya, a five-star all-inclusive resort on the beach at Playa del

Carmen. Located on Mexico's Yucatan peninsula on the Gulf of Mexico, the resort looked like the Taj Mahal, surrounded by tall, swaying palms. Lined with luscious landscaping and sparkling pools, the courtyard was beautiful and a relaxing place to gather. For the families that attended, the resort served as tropical retreat and an exhilarating change of pace. We spent hours playing water volleyball in the pool and beaching along the Playa de Carmen. Our dinners were set in a festive street atmosphere at a table for 20. Oddly, my previous business partner with MBA and the dealers who had chosen to stay with MBA happened to be having their incentive trip the same weekend at a nearby resort, but that was not going to stop me from enjoying Mattress Direct's inaugural incentive trip.

The trip had been a rejuvenating experience for all of us. However, Chloe hinted that she would have preferred more luxurious accommodations. However, for the leadership team, the dealers, and myself, we all felt as if we were vacationing in paradise. Now I consider myself to be more of a "go with the flow" type of guy, while my wife had more of a "take-charge" personality. This was apparent when our group, dressed in matching T-shirts embellished with their names or nicknames on them, was assembling for the "famous" group photo. My prerogative was to let everyone naturally congregate for the photo. They could be standing up, sitting down, blocking each other. It did not matter. My wife, however, chose to direct everyone as to where and how they should pose. I let her take the lead, as I am a laid-back type of person, but it later became apparent that she wanted to direct more than the photo shoot. Toward the end of the trip, as we were riding to the airport on the shuttle bus, still reeling from that magical week, Chloe embarrassed me in front of my entire team. She made it known, in front of everyone, that she did not like my leadership style and proceeded to tell me how to improve it. To be fair to my wife, she had just finished her yoga teacher certification, which emphasized giving feedback. I do not think she was purposely trying to be critical, but her comments hurt my ego and brought me down a few notches.

Aside from our personality differences, the legal difficulties due to the Mattress Direct lawsuit were also taking a toll on our marriage. We had been married just about one year when I had filed for bankruptcy, which, I am sure, from her perspective, must have been stressful. The lawsuit negatively affected our relationship, as it would any marriage. When I came home from work, Chloe always wanted to know the details of the case. It felt as if I was being interrogated by attorneys during the day, and in the evenings, by my wife. The stress she must have felt from the lawsuit was not her fault. After all, I would not say that I was the best communicator when it came to discussing the legal details. Still, I felt a lot of pressure at home and felt as if I needed to escape. So, when I was invited to go on a skiing trip with two of my friends and my friend's brother that spring, I did not hesitate to go. Taking a trip without my wife was not something I would usually do, but I needed some time away. While I was away on the ski trip, I had such a great time with my buddies that I realized I could be away from my wife and still have fun.

So, after I was served with the injunction against Mattress Direct, it was not difficult for me to make the decision to leave Florida, at least for the time being. I packed a few belongings and bought a one-way airplane ticket to Michigan, leaving my marriage troubles and the business I was no longer able to legally run behind.

Michigan is comprised of two peninsulas, the upper and the lower. The coastal land masses, large and small, jut into Lake Michigan on the western side with Lake Huron to the east. Bellaire, located on the northern side of the lower peninsula, was my destination. Mom and Pops owned one of the oldest homes in the village with a population of less than 1,200 people. They had bought and renovated the Antrim County residence, which was built in 1890, a nearly 2,500-square foot home with two bedrooms and two bathrooms located on two acres at the intersection of West Cayuga Street and North Bridge Street. My mom had renovated the downstairs and started an antique business, Mr. and Mrs. B's Mercantile, Ltd. Several apartments were located upstairs, which is where I would be staying. On the wooded property was a gazebo, a front porch, and an historic barn. Nearby were forests and rivers, bays and lakes. The village was so peaceful and quiet, so different from Jacksonville, the state of Florida's most populous city with nearly 1,000,000 residents. When I arrived in mid-May, Michigan was still experiencing springtime weather with temperatures in the mid-60's, a refreshing change from Florida's already summertime heat.

I arrived at the airport and rented a car because my parents were still back in Ohio. Mom would not be coming to Michigan for a couple of days. Pops was still working at Boutselis Auto Care in Columbus, which he had owned and operated for years. When I pulled the rental car into the driveway, there was a man at the property making some repairs to the roof. He came down from the ladder, extended a hand, and introduced himself as the handyman.

"You must be Darren," he said. "I'm Sam. I live across the street." We talked for a short while until he indicated he needed to get back to work. During our conversation he had inadvertently mentioned, via code word, that there were recovery meetings every Wednesday night, and that I was welcome to attend if I wanted to. How had he known? We had only talked for a few minutes. I thanked him for his kind offer then let myself into the house and gave my parents a call to let them know I had arrived safely.

Now that I was settled in, I decided to have a look around Mom's antique store. It was beautifully decorated and a testimony to all things vintage and antique. There was furniture, glassware, china, knick knacks, lamps, art, tablecloths, doilies, black and white photographs, and other home accessories. Mom was a bit of a pack rat, but in a good way. She had a good eye and was always doing something creative. We did, however, have different ideas about how to run a business. Mom was an intelligent woman who knew the value of the items in her store, but she would not lower her prices. I wanted to help her clean out her inventory, so I lowered the prices just enough so that she would still make a profit.

After a few days, Mom arrived. She was happy that I had cleaned out the antique store, but we never did see eye to eye on the pricing. It was great catching up with her, but after a couple of weeks, I started to feel confined. The village of Bellaire was small and hardly populated, and that was something I was not accustomed to. In Jacksonville, I was attending recovery meetings with a lot of people, but in Bellaire, there were only four or five people including myself! Plus, I was used to going to a yoga studio now and then but there were none to be found locally.

I decided to keep the rental car and do some discovering outside of Bellaire. The small towns and cities that flanked the northwestern tip of the lower peninsula, some twenty to thirty miles north or south of Bellaire, were filled with history. One of my favorite places to visit was Charlevoix. The town's best kept secret was the Earl Young Mushroom homes, which looked like mushrooms or Hobbit homes. There were 31 in all, and each architectural design was unique. Made of limestone, fieldstone, and heavy, massive boulders, the smaller homes were cottages while the larger ones looked like mansions with wavy roofs. Traverse City, the largest city in northern Michigan, had its share of interesting historical buildings, and the city of Petoskey, a small coastal town on Little Traverse Bay was a beautiful place to visit.

My parents rarely took a day off. It seemed as if they did not believe in taking vacations, which is why I asked Mom if she wanted to spend the day with me, and, to my surprise, she said "yes". I picked the destination: Beaver Island, the largest island in Lake Michigan with a population of around 500. We drove 45 minutes from Bellaire up the western coast of Michigan to Charlevoix. Instead of taking the two-hour ferry to Beaver Island, we opted to take a four-seater Beechcraft prop plane for a flight over the deep blue waters of northern Lake Michigan. From there, all the eyes could see was the expanse of the heavily wooded island outlined by a sea of blue. Mom got a kick out of the plane ride and even took a selfie of us, which she saved to her cell phone! After ten short minutes, we landed on the island. The airport was tiny and looked like a little shack.

Because Mom had suffered a stroke awhile back, we did most of our sight-seeing by car. I rented a very small car similar to a VW rabbit. We drove around the 14-mile-long island, which was 7 miles at its widest, visiting shops, and touring the historical sites and the lighthouse. Neither of us knew that Beaver Island had once had a "king." James Strang, a Mormon, had brought his followers with him to this Irish-populated island before the U.S. Civil War occurred due to religious persecution. Some of the woods were cleared to make an internal road called the King's highway. Strang, a polygamist, had five wives and 14 children, and was voted into the Michigan House of Representatives twice during the 1850's. Unfortunately, due to his harsh tactics among his own people as well as those who did not follow him, he was not well liked. He was fatally shot in the back in 1856. Strangely, the murderers were never charged.

As we spent the day touring the island, the skies had grown cloudy, and the winds cooled. Once we made it back to the airport, the pilot told us we might be stuck on Beaver Island for the night due to the weather, but then at the last minute, he changed his mind, and we flew back to Charlevoix where I took Mom to dinner. I felt that the day had been magical. I just enjoyed listening to her tell me about what her life was like, what her dreams were, what she did as a child. It felt good to be present and listen to her with no distractions. No phone. No T.V. Just me and my mom hanging out.

I had started to enjoy my visit to Michigan, but there were some days when I felt numb. I was far away from my home in Florida. Unable to do business. Not knowing if my marriage was going to survive. But I did not want to feel broken, nor did I want to think of myself as a man who had failed. Instead of reacting in a negative way, I decided to just sit back and enjoy the ride, which might have seemed counterintuitive, but it worked. When I had started my road to recovery from alcoholism years back in 2008, one of the most important things I had learned was that my plan was not necessarily the plan that needed to be executed. Instead, I needed to follow God's plan, always different from my plan, and always the better plan.

Chapter Three

"Have you started any other companies since you left Mattress by Appointment?" one of the opposing attorneys asked me.

"I don't think so," I answered. I paused momentarily, suddenly realizing that my answer might have sounded a bit shaky. Technically, I had not "started" any companies. I had, however, registered a marketing company called Marketing Direct, but I had never funded it or even launched it. Marketing Direct was not a viable company. It had nothing to do with the mattress industry. I was an entrepreneur at heart. My mind was always spinning with new and creative ways to do business. Marketing Direct was not a "company." It had merely been an "idea."

I had flown back from Michigan to Jacksonville for the deposition only to find myself sitting in the "hot" seat and feeling quite uncomfortable doing so. For 18 hours over several days, the opposing attorneys found ways to repeatedly ask me the same questions in different ways. Having to constantly be on guard was not only physically exhausting, but it was also emotionally draining. I felt as if I was being interrogated by a prosecutor like a criminal who was on trial for his life.

As I continued to talk, the video camera situated across the long boardroom table continued to record my deposition. To my left were the opposing attorneys. To my right was my attorney and a court reporter. A judge was not present.

My attorney looked at me and raised an eyebrow. "Hey, we need to take a break," he interjected. I was no longer working with C.F. I had decided to hire an up-and-coming lawyer, who had been highly recommended to me by a long-time colleague. When I first met the young, well-dressed man a few months ago, he had shown a lot of enthusiasm about the case and believed that we could win.

The attorneys sitting around the table agreed to take a break. My lawyer signaled for me to follow him. We walked down a nondescript hallway until we reached a conference room with only a few chairs and a table in it. He shut the door behind us, making sure that no one would hear our conversation. "Hey, you committed perjury," he said in a whispered tone. "You have to change what you just said, or I can't represent you any longer."

Perjury? That was a strong word. I was not lying about starting up another company. I could feel in my gut that my attorney was backing out of this case although I was not sure why.

Although my lawyer's remarks were unexpected and a complete shock, I decided that I was not going to change my answer. I had not started another company. That was the truth. As we walked back to the boardroom in silence, I was fuming. The interrogation continued until 5 p.m. that day but I kept my peace.

I walked to the parking lot feeling drained and defeated. I unlocked the door to my Yukon Denali XL, which had originally been my wife's car, and drove back to the house. Even though I did not particularly like driving the big bus, I had sold my car and taken over her payments, so that she could get a vehicle that was more affordable for her. Back at the house I packed my belongings, mostly clothes, photographs, and my computer, said my goodbyes to Chloe, then called out to my nine-year-old yellow lab, Buddy, tail wagging and jumping eagerly into the front passenger seat. I locked the doors, put the keys in the ignition, and hit the gas pedal. With my marriage, my home, and my business now in the rearview mirror, I was ready to move on, the destination, once again, Bellaire, Michigan. It only seemed logical to me that I should go back to Bellaire. The Fourth of July was soon approaching and it was a family tradition to spend the holiday together no matter where we would be spending it.

I merged onto I-95 North and found myself fighting the rush hour traffic. Buddy, tongue hanging out, watched the cars, trucks, and landscape fly by. As we finally reached the Jacksonville city limits and headed toward the Florida-Georgia border, I realized that my marriage to Chloe was probably over. My wife had been a comfort to me three years ago when my little brother passed away. At the time, her kindness and compassion had attracted me like a bee to a wildflower. In looking back, I recognized that I had just jumped into the relationship headfirst with my eyes closed. Instead of "Aim. Fire. Ready," I was more of a "Fire. Aim. Ready!" type of guy. Chloe and I got along. We did not argue. There was no drama or trauma due to us going our separate ways. We just both recognized that neither of us could overcome the many challenges that we were both currently facing. I could not give her the security she needed, being one million dollars in debt, and she was not giving me the love and support that I needed to get through this trial.

Buddy and I continued driving in Georgia, passing through Brunswick and historical Savannah, the traffic flowing as we crossed into South Carolina. We veered west onto I-26 and headed toward the state capitol of Columbia. From there, Buddy and I had another 100 miles to drive before reaching our first stop: Anderson, South Carolina.

Anderson was where Scott Andrew, the CEO and owner of RSS, lived with his wife, Daphene. When I called Scott to tell him I would be driving through his neck of the woods hoping we could meet, both he and his wife extended a warm invitation to visit them at their home. I had met with Scott in person a few times over the past several years, ironically, due to the numerous legal challenges we both faced with PMD albeit for different reasons. We first met in 2008, when he was working as a dealer with PMD. He was about to file a lawsuit against the company and had asked me to write an affidavit on his behalf, even though I had left PMD five years prior.

Six years later, in 2014, I met with Scott again, this time on a layover at the Atlanta airport on my way back home to Jacksonville. During our brief meeting, he shared his vision of his multi-level business plan with me and expressed that he would like to go into business together. The opportunity sounded attractive, but I was more focused on building a duplicatable mattress company with my business partner at the time, ironically, the partner who had taken over MBA who was now suing me for starting Mattress Direct.

Before I pulled into the driveway of the Andrews' beautiful lake home in Anderson, I double-checked my GPS to make sure I had the right place. Before I even got out of the car,

Scott and Daphene came outside to greet me and welcome me with open arms. We spent the day leisurely, enjoying their expansive backyard with a pool, cooking steaks and crab on the grill. The couple had two dogs: an intimidating black German Shepherd named Bo, and a white Great Pyrenees named Sammy. Out of consideration for Buddy, they kept the dogs penned up.

That day Scott offered me part-ownership of RSS once the lawsuit with MBA was settled. In return, I would help RSS streamline its processes and build a viable dealer community. What this meant was that I would be giving RSS my playbook in advance. Obviously, this kind of arrangement would only work if I trusted Scott would keep his promise. Remember, at this time, I was not permitted to work in the industry for one year. Working with RSS in the future, however, felt like my only option. If I did not, I would lose everything I had built the past 15 years.

Scott was still suing me to collect on the judgement he had been awarded from PMD. He was following legal procedure. Legalities aside, that did not change the fact that my bank accounts had been drained. In an attempt to keep MBA, I had to file for bankruptcy because I had "zero" financial assets. While this strategy seemed like a good idea at the time, it did not work. I lost the company to my previous business partner. So, before I left the Andrews' home that day, Scott promised that he would make things right again. He even called my parents and explained that he would fix everything.

At the time, RSS was a small company with 18 dealers, mostly big furniture store owners. I advised Scott that creating small, duplicatable mattress showrooms would help the company grow exponentially. The plan was to establish a simple, cookie-cutter foundation. Once that foundation was cemented, the dealers could always expand their businesses into larger stores if they so wished, or they could choose to remain as small stores. Regardless of the size of the store, the underlying foundation would remain the same. Scott received my advice with interest, although I am sure he thought the idea sounded a bit unconventional, most likely, due to its simplicity.

That night, with my stomach full and my mind hopeful for the future, I slept soundly in Scott and Daphene's guestroom. My visit had been productive, at least in establishing the foundation of what could become a great business relationship in the future. I knew that it would take time for this to come to fruition, but how long it would take, I did not know. I just had to remain with the flow and let life lead me in the right direction. In the morning, I awoke feeling bright and hopeful. I thanked Scott and Daphene once again for their hospitality before heading back out onto the road, feeling optimistic about the future and this potential, newfound direction.

Heading north on I-26, Buddy and I had nearly a 500-mile journey through the mountains ahead of us. Our next stop was Columbus, Ohio, my hometown and also the location of RSS headquarters. But I would not be visiting either place. Instead, I would be visiting a previous PMD colleague of mine named Jerry Williams, who was now the COO of RSS. Jerry and I had been members of the same fraternity at Ohio State University but not at the same time. He had graduated a few years before I did. We had not spoken since I left PMD in 2003. Rather than a meet-and-greet, our meeting would be more like a reunion as well as a way for me to learn more about RSS.

We drove through Asheville, North Carolina, famous for its furniture manufacturers, then continued north through

Johnson City and Kingsport in Tennessee. We passed through the western tip of Virginia, and the state of Kentucky, then Huntington, West Virginia, which lies on the southern border of the Ohio River, a wide, winding body of water that clearly designates the southern Ohio border. As we reached Chillicothe, Ohio, we only had a 45-mile drive north to Columbus, the state capital and the most populous city in the Buckeye state. It felt good to be back in my home state again. It was a familiar place, the place where I grew up. There is something to be said about the state of Ohio and Ohioans. We have a common history, a common root. No matter how far away we move. No matter how long it has been since we have talked to one another. These roots are the keepers of our memories. They connect us to one another, and they always bring us back.

I plugged Jerry's address into my GPS. It did not take long for us to arrive. After parking the car, it felt good to get out and stretch my legs. I imagined that Buddy must have felt the same way too as he shook himself off, wagged his tail, and sniffed the lawn. I knocked on the door, and a familiar face answered. It was a smiling face, a face that had not aged over the years. Jerry invited us inside and we settled down. We started talking, catching up on the happenings of the past ten years while the hours flew by. We talked about Ohio State football, our college years, our families. Then, the subject of RSS came up. Jerry had a way of calming me down in the toughest of situations. He alleviated my concerns about working with RSS and expressed that he felt positive about his experiences in working with Scott. Jerry's testimony that day was the reason I decided to become a part of RSS. He was and still is a loyal, honest, and genuinely good guy that anyone would want to have as a part of their team. He was aware of the current rumors that were circulating about my role with PMD and he knew that they were untrue. Jerry told me that Scott was convinced of this as well because he had reviewed my track record with the previous mattress companies I had created and built, including Carolina Bedding, Carolina Bedding Direct, Mattress by Appointment, and Mattress Direct.

Buddy and I stayed at Jerry's house that night. The next morning, we headed to Bellaire. We had a little more than a six-hour drive ahead of us with the sweet destination of coming home to family. We hopped onto I-75 north, driving through Toledo, Ohio, then Ann Arbor, Michigan, which lies on the western outskirts of Detroit. The sun was brightly shining, the temperature was comfortable, and I was still feeling optimistic. Heading north past Flint and Saginaw, we would arrive within the hour. It was now time to forget about business and focus on spending time with my parents, my younger brother John, and our family friends. I was revved up on good vibes and pure faith. To keep this positive momentum going, I only needed two things: patience and time. Time would bring me patience, and patience, I was sure, would help me bide my time.

Chapter Four

The tip of Lake Bellaire came into view as my brother John and I descended the winding road from my parents' log cabin. I had just returned from a recovery meeting, picked up John, then hopped back in the car so we could spend the Fourth of July together fishing and swimming. Our plan was to pick up our watercraft from our parents' lake house and ride to Torch Lake, a deep inland lake and Michigan's second largest.

The 19-mile lake, just south of Charlevoix and Petoskey, is separated from Lake Michigan by just a sliver of land. Like the Great Lakes, Torch Lake was carved by ancient ice age glaciers. With its crystal-clear turquoise waters, due to its limestone bottom, and pure white sandbars lining its shores, Torch Lake looked like a scene from Tahiti. Long ago, the Native Americans who traversed the lake with birchbark canoes named it "Torch Lake" because they used torches to find fish.

This year was the first time we would be getting together as a family at the log cabin for the Fourth of July. In years past, we spent many Christmases there. The cabin sits on a 10-acre tract of forest on the highest peak of the Shanty Creek Ski Resort near Bellaire. Custom-built in 1998 during my younger brothers' growing-up years, the two-story cabin, which resembles a Swiss chalet, is constructed from massive logs of northern pine. Whenever my younger brothers and I stayed there, we hung out in our "man cave" in the basement, or lowest floor of the cabin, the same level as the three-car garage. Our bunk room literally looked like a cave. It had eight giant log cabin-style bunks, a shower, and a mud room where we could store our ski gear and our fishing gear. We always slept on the lower bunks, reserving the upper ones for guests. To get to the main floor, a stairway led to the great room which had vaulted ceilings, a fireplace, and a large glass window offering spectacular views of the woods. The wrap-around deck was the perfect place for barbeques. It was peaceful there. Secluded and quiet.

"Hey, John. Remember that time you took me snowboarding?" I laughed as we were nearing the lake house.

"Yeah. That lasted all of five minutes."

That was Christmas 2008, about a month after I became sober. My younger brothers, who were much more experienced snowboarders than me, asked me to join them and their friends. In fact, I had never gone snowboarding before. But that did not matter. I knew how to ski. In fact, I was a more experienced skier than my brothers. How hard could it be to balance on a board rather than two skis? I was always up for a new adventure and it sounded like a lot of fun. *Hitting the slopes with my little brothers. Racing down the hill. Laughing all the way down.* When my brothers were younger, we always played a game called "I'm better." Because I was so much older, I usually won! I have always had a competitive spirit, and our games were always fun. Now that my brothers had grown up, there was definitely more competition. They already owned their own snowboards. I had to rent one. After gearing up, we got on the lift. By the time we made it to the top, my brothers and their friends had taken off and were ahead of me. Racing to catch up. I leaned too much into the turn and fell flat on my face. I got up, dusted myself off, but my hand was throbbing. The only thing I could do was pick up the board and walk down the hill with dignity and my head held high. I ended up breaking my finger, so I put a splint on it and then rented some skis.

"Yeah. Well, at least I got some good skiing in that day," I laughed. My brothers and I always liked to joke around.

When my brother John was born, I was 18 years old. One and one-half years later, my brother Dan came into the world. Just two weeks before his 22nd birthday, Dan tragically passed away. His death was traumatic for our family, but it brought all of us closer together. This year, the 14th of July, would be the third anniversary of Dan's passing.

I thought about the night I got the call. I was at home with my fiancée Chloe watching late night comedy. My cell phone rang. It was Pops. He rarely called me, and it was unusually late for a call.

"Darren!"

I knew something was wrong. His voice sounded shaky.

"Dan is gone. He passed away. John found him. He was in his room…"

"What happened?"

I already knew the answer to that question. My brother Dan liked to party and was struggling with street drugs. I felt weak and sick to my stomach. I could see Chloe out of the corner of my eye. She had lowered the volume on the T.V.

I walked to the massive glass windows overlooking the night ocean. *I was worried about John finding Dan like that. And Mom. What about Mom?*

"Is John okay?" I asked my dad.

I watched as each wave crested then crashed onto the shore. The dark sky had blended into the water, revealing only the white tips of the waves as they rolled in. I remembered when Dan had first visited me here. He had bought a surfboard and headed out to catch some waves. It did not matter to him that he did not know how to surf. He was out there trying, even after his body was being tossed about this way and that in the ocean. To me, Dan was invincible. But now he was gone. I loved Dan so much. All I wanted to do at that moment was die. I wanted to die so I could see Dan again.

After I hung up with Pops, Chloe and I took a walk on the beach. It felt comforting to feel the wind on my face and her hand in mine. "I'm going with you to Ohio," she whispered. "For the funeral. You shouldn't go alone." I immediately felt loved and cared for. At that moment, she became my lifeline.

Hundreds of people came to Dan's wake. Family members. Friends. Dan's fraternity brothers from Sigma Phi Epsilon at Jacksonville University, many of whom came to pay their last respects from out of state. During the funeral, the priest asked our family to stand by the casket and pay our last respects. Chloe was seated on a small couch. My parents had never met her before but motioned for her to join us. She approached the casket with reverence and held my hand like an angel. I was so touched by her caring and concern that I proposed to her two months later. At our wedding reception, we set a place for Dan so he could be with us. Now, just two years later, our marriage was over, but I did not feel sad. I knew that Chloe would be okay without me. She was an independent woman.

"Hey, Darren," John said, waking me from my thoughts.

"Yeah, bro."

"That Grizzly Bear you picked up today. That was awesome. I know Dan would have loved it. Mom and Dad sure did."

At the recovery meeting that morning in Central Lake, there was a guy in the parking lot using a blow torch, which is not something one would usually see. On the bed of his truck, cigarette in mouth, he used the torch to put the final touches on a three-foot high wooden sculpture of a Grizzly bear. The bear seemed to be looking directly at me as he stood upright on his hind feet clutching his front paws in front of his chest. I pulled out my wallet and bought the carving. When I got back to the cabin, I placed it outside in remembrance of my brother Dan.

John and I pulled into the lake house. It was still being renovated. We walked to the floating dock that was attached to the bottom of the lake with a 20-foot chain. I could smell the scent of Muskgrass lining the shore. Lake Bellaire, once called Grass Lake, due to its grassy shoreline, was cold and deep and a great place to fish for walleye, bass, and sunfish, lake trout, perch, and crappie. John hopped into the boat, and I followed him in the wave runner. We rode along the marshes to Grass River, a narrow, two-mile waterway bordered by rich green grass and trees. From there we traversed Clam Lake, a shallow lake that flows into Torch Lake. All in all, the trip would take about 45 minutes.

I like to think of Torch Lake as one of Michigan's best kept secrets, but that year, thousands of visitors spent the Fourth of July weekend there. That year, 2015, set the precedent for taming the lake parties for the next couple of years. Despite the crowds, John and I spent the day fishing, swimming, and diving at my parent's friends' house on Torch Lake, Art and Joannie. Joannie had been my dad's college girlfriend and they were still friends. Her husband Art was a dentist. We had lunch at their place before heading back to pick up our parents. Then, in the evening, we went to Art and Joannie's other house on Lake Michigan for a cookout, bonfire, and fireworks show. John and I went all out on the fireworks, lighting at least ten mortars at a time, filling the sky over the lake with color and light for hours. As a grand finale, we lit paper lanterns in Dan's memory, watching them glow as they floated into the night sky. We spent the rest of night laughing, singing songs, and telling stories by the bonfire.

A few days later, my parents and brother left for Ohio, and Buddy went along with them. My mom was ecstatic to have Buddy as her new companion, and I knew she would take care of him and give him a good home. I was thankful for everything my parents did for me and wanted to return the favor by staining their log cabin for them. The job had to be done every two years, and it would be expensive for them to hire a professional. I stayed on at the cabin, instead of at the apartment in town, so that I could work on it a little bit each day. I also did not have any income due to my legal troubles, so they offered to pay me for the work. I still was paying the mortgage on my condo in Florida and helping Chloe financially as we were still married.

So, every morning, for a few hours, I would arm myself with a ladder, a paintbrush, and a bucket of stain. Working outside in the summer sun was rejuvenating. The weather is temperate during the Michigan summers. But, after working on the cabin for a few days, I realized it would not be as easy as I had thought. First of all, it was a two-story cabin. There were just certain places, due to the height of the expansive house, that I would not be able to reach. I also definitely avoided the beehive! Not only that, it was also hard to see where I had previously done the staining. Staining a log cabin is like putting clear paint on a white wall. Once it dries, it disappears.

When I was not working on the cabin, I was attending recovery meetings, working out, and planting the seeds for my future work with RSS, even though I was not on the payroll yet. My mind was always active, thinking of ways to unify all of the dealers under one roof, so to speak. I started by creating a private Facebook group where the dealers could logon to obtain information, assistance, tips, and training. I also created an automated leaderboard with up-to-date data because it was crucial to growing momentum. People like to see how they rank with others. It builds friendly competition between stores and it motivates people to work harder. Ways to make the first RSS national incentive trip a time to remember were also in the works. The incentive trips not only rewarded successful dealers, but they were also a way for dealers to meet one another as well as the leadership team. Incentive trips were a great way to learn how to improve the business and socialize at the same time, and they were also fun.

Yes, I had given RSS my game plan without any guarantee that I would be an owner of the company in the future. But I had an innate trust and faith that I would be. I also did not believe that I was giving away my game plan haphazardly. No, giving Scott the game plan was like sowing seeds that would yield a bountiful crop. I just had to take that first step and believe. At times, however, I felt like the stain painted onto those exterior cabin walls. Invisible. But I also knew that I was laying the important groundwork for the company sight unseen, hoping to make it stronger and viable, whether I was a part of its future or not.

Chapter Five

By the end of July, I was ready to leave Michigan. My parents and my brother John had returned to Ohio weeks ago, and I had stayed by myself at the cabin. When I left Florida one month ago, I had been thinking about taking a cross-country road trip. It was something I have always dreamed about doing but never had the time. Well, now I had a lot of time on my hands. Coming back to Michigan gave me the chance to reset myself emotionally and it also helped me to get financially stabilized. The amount of money my parents gave me to stain the cabin set me up for the next four months, enabling me to pay the mortgage and make Chloe's car payment. She was still my wife and I felt responsible, both morally and legally, for her well-being.

Chloe and I were married on May 4, 2013. It was the second marriage for both of us and my first wedding celebration. Sometime before the wedding, I had a conversation with a friend who had lost a sibling. One practice that helped her grieve, she said, was meditating. She would sit quietly, close her eyes, and breathe slowly and deeply. When she felt completely relaxed, she would try to align with her brother's energy. "Please give me a word," she would say. This seemed to comfort her, and, while I found her idea interesting, I did not put it into practice until several months later. A few days before the wedding, I had to pick up the flowers. I had been thinking about my brother Dan and how he would not be here to celebrate with us. I pulled the car into the parking lot and turned the ignition off. But something was stopping me from going inside the florist shop. I stayed in the car observing what was going on around me. There was a lot of traffic that day. The parking lot was filled with people walking to and from the stores, packages being delivered by delivery trucks, and cars racing about. I closed my eyes and listened to the humming of the traffic, an occasional police siren, the opening and closing of car doors, footsteps. Eventually, I was able to block out the noise and focus on my breathing. Then, I remembered the advice my friend had given me. "Dan," I whispered. "Dan, if you're here…." A smile came across my face just thinking about him. I saw him as a baby; how tiny he was. I saw him during his growing up years playing and goofing around, then his college years, staying with me at my condo in Florida before heading off to school.

"If you can hear me, Dan. Just give me a word." I sat patiently and listened and waited for a word. And then, I heard it.

Grizzly! Yes, grizzly.

At 6'4" and 240 pounds, Dan towered over most people, including me. My brother was big, burly, and athletic. If anyone was a Grizzly bear, it was my brother Dan. Dan also was fond of chewing tobacco and, Grizzly had been his favorite brand.

Yes, "grizzly" was the word that Dan had given me.

The word had started with the wooden carving of the Grizzly bear I had brought home from a recovery meeting in Bellaire, which was now a permanent fixture outside of our family's log cabin home. I remember how excited I was when I brought it back to the cabin, placing it in front of the door and knocking. "Surprise! Look who came to visit us, Mom," I said smiling as she answered the door.

My brother Dan had given me the word and I was ready to leave both Florida and Michigan behind and venture on a cross-country road trip. I did not have any firm plans in mind with the exception of heading west and meeting with a few friends and acquaintances along the way. My first stop would be Madison, Wisconsin, where I was planning on meeting with Joel, a long-time friend and business colleague, and now the national recruiter for RSS. The purpose of the meeting was to reconnect with him face-to-face and establish trust. Even though he was a loyal friend and we had known each other for more than 20 years, I was still "technically" a competitor.

I cleaned up the cabin, packed up my belongings, and got on the road in order to reach the ferry on time. It would be a one and one-half hour drive to Ludington, Michigan, where I would set sail across Lake Michigan on the S.S. Badger. With its surface area of 22,404 square feet, Lake Michigan is a massive body of water, at its maximum width 118 miles and at its longest, 307 miles, bordering Wisconsin, Illinois, Indiana, and Michigan. It is sometimes referred to as the third ocean of the United States, in addition to the Atlantic and the Pacific, due to its blue waters and white beaches. Taking the ferry instead of driving only made sense. I would be avoiding a 15-hour drive around Lake Michigan. That is just how big the lake is!

The S.S. Badger has been traversing the waters of Lake Michigan since the early 1950's. For nearly thirty years, the steamship, which looked more like the Titanic, transported railway cars. When that mission had been accomplished, a retired entrepreneur purchased the boat in 1990 and started the passenger and vehicle ferry that is still in operation today. The ship, now an icon, was entered into the national historic register in 2016. Cruising at an average speed of 18 miles per hour, the S.S. Badger makes the 62-mile trip across Lake Michigan from Ludington, Michigan to Manitowoc, Wisconsin in about four hours. The seven-story ferry has one deck for vehicles and two decks for passengers including 40 staterooms. I booked a small stateroom, with a small bed and a bathroom for $49. I spent my time strolling along the deck and catching a glimpse of the sun glistening on the lake waters. It was fun and relaxing.

As I was doing so, I met two ladies and we started up a conversation. Whenever I meet someone new, I enjoy learning about their background, where they are from, what they do. One of the ladies, Joann, who looked about my mom's age, happened to be from Canal Winchester, which is where my parents lived and my brothers grew up. Joann's daughter was coincidentally from Petoskey, which is also close to Bellaire. Obviously, Joann and I had a geographical connection, but there was something more to it. She had such a positive outlook on life. Her energy radiated warmth and kindness. I instantly felt a connection with her and felt comfortable telling her about my cross-country journey. I also shared how I was currently going through a divorce, even though neither I nor Chloe had filed papers yet. Joann and her friend consoled me by saying that I would have "no problem finding someone new." Joann wanted to introduce me to her daughter! Even though I was travelling by myself, I did not feel alone. I knew that there would be plenty of people to meet along the way, good people, like Joann.

I spent the morning enjoying the ship, checking out the game room and the restaurant in addition to taking in the beautiful views. The Michigan summers are gorgeous. There is something about being up north that makes the skies bluer, the breezes calmer, the water clearer. By the time we docked in Manitowoc, Wisconsin, I was ready for my meeting with Joel. Joel was a tall, Nordic-looking man, and was 6'4" like my brother Dan. Although we did not know each other at the time, we both had worked for Vector Marketing selling Cutco knives when we were in our twenties. We actually met a few years later when we were regional coordinators for CollegeClub.com, which was kind of like a modern-day Facebook for students. As coordinators, our role was to hire college-aged students to promote the website. Joel and I had met at one of the quarterly meetings in San Diego and had been friends ever since.

I greeted Joel with a handshake and a smile. When I meet with others, my goal is to establish a good rapport and build trust. I could not wait to share my future vision for RSS with Joel. My goal was to help the company grow via community-building and state-of-the-art training. Just because I was not permitted to work in the mattress industry for one year did not mean I could not think about how I would be making a comeback in the future.

Joel and I decided to grab a bite to eat then visit the furniture store he co-owned with Jerry Moore, an RSS dealer, in Pewaukee, Wisconsin. Driving to Pewaukee would require a bit of backtracking on my part, as the city is on the western outskirts of Milwaukee. But seeing the store and meeting with Joel and Jerry was important. Joel told Jerry about my role as a regional founder of their current business model, a by-appointment style model. Jerry's store differed in that the furniture was kept in a large furniture warehouse instead of a small shop. I shared some of my advertising strategies, and my philosophies about the simple, duplicatable business model, my area of expertise. After our brief meeting, we parted ways so I could hop on I-90 west before it got dark. My goal was to drive about six hours per day so I would also have some time for sight-seeing or meetings. After passing through the city of Lacrosse, Wisconsin's westernmost city, I crossed the Mississippi River into Minnesota, driving until I reached farm country near the town of High Forest, where I looked for a roadside hotel on the interstate for a place to spend the night.

Morning came quickly. A man feels like he can change the world after having a good night's sleep and a great cup of coffee. I was excited and felt recharged, so different than I had felt a little more than a month ago, even more than a day ago. I was ready for another day of adventure on I-90 when I passed a sign that read "Blue Earth Exit 1 mile." There was no way I was going to pass this little town and not stop by. The name sounded cool, and I thought it would make for good conversation someday in the future. I pulled onto the main drag and drove into the downtown area. The township of Blue Earth got its name from the river surrounding it, the Blue Earth River, known for its copper-containing blue-green clay. As I passed the Blue Earth Truck stop, a towering statue of the Jolly Green Giant, so known for its advertising on cans of vegetables throughout the years, emerged from between the trees. I smiled for thinking of Dan, who, as I said at 6'4", very much looked like a giant. I turned onto Giant Drive, and pulled into the Jolly Green Giant Statuary Park, snapping a few pictures then heading straight back to the highway. When I was pulling out of the park, a Ford Mustang passed me by. How my brother Dan loved mustangs! I wish he could have been here with me to see all of this! I continued driving, pulling into the turn lane to merge onto the interstate when a 12-point buck ran directly in front of the Denali. Luckily, we did not make contact! I started laughing uncontrollably, thinking of the deer scene from the movie *Tommy Boy*, the one where Chris Farley (Tommy) and David Spade (Richie) get freaked out when a deer (that they thought was dead) in the backseat of their car wakes up, demolishes the car, and runs away. My brothers and I loved that movie. If there was one thing about my brothers and me, we were always joking around and laughing. We had such a tight connection. I thought about Dan again, his personality a combination of Chris Farley, David Spade, Will Ferrell, Vince Vaughn, and John C. Reilly. And, then it hit me. I realized what had been happening all along! There was more to this road trip than just driving across the country and meeting people along the way. My brother Dan had been giving me signs that he had been here with me all along, right here in the front passenger seat.

Chapter Six

As I was driving west on I-90 toward South Dakota, I reached into my cooler and grabbed a bottle of the cold stuff. I had made 40 to 50 bottles of it since leaving Michigan, and the cooler was still well-stocked. In each bottle was my recipe for health: cold-pressed juice made from a concoction of celery, spinach, green apples, parsley, ginger, and lemon juice. I have always been a health-conscious individual and truly believe that you are what you eat, or, in this case, drink.

A documentary called *Fat, Sick, and Nearly Dead,* the story of Joe Cross, an Australian man who was "100 pounds overweight, loaded up on steroids and suffering from a debilitating autoimmune disease," had touched me. Knowing that his health was putting his life in danger, Joe came to America and travelled across the country, from New York City to San Diego, consuming green juice for 60 days to regain his health. If he could make such a trip, I could as well. Joe Cross's journey made me feel in alignment with my own cross-country adventure.

I had scored a free juicer from Jerry Williams. When we met in Columbus, the topic of juicing had come up during our conversation. Jerry joked that he was only using his to make margaritas! Now, I am well aware that a plant-based diet is much healthier than a meat and potatoes diet. I eat meat—I am not vegan or vegetarian—and I believe that juicing is healthy. I also fast 19 hours a day, only eating between 5 p.m. and 10 p.m., a practice called intermittent fasting. But again, I am never rigid in my practices. There are times when I break my own self-imposed rules. If I need to, or have to, I will eat outside of those times. I consider myself to be the opposite of "rigid."

I had already driven hundreds of miles since leaving Michigan with no real plan or destination in mind other than landing somewhere in the vicinity of San Diego. I did have a friend who had recently moved from Jacksonville Beach to Carlsbad to open a high-end fitness clothing store, a lady I had met through Chloe in the yoga community. Once I got to California, I planned on calling her and connecting. When I met Katie awhile back, we had an instant bond. First of all, her parents, like mine, grew up in Ohio. Secondly, one of her parents went to Upper Ellington High School and the other attended West High School, the same schools that my mom and dad respectively attended. That could not be a coincidence.

I continued driving west on I-90. Crossing the Missouri River, stopping in Oacoma, a small town on the western banks which had been "established in 1891 as a stopping-off place for explorers, fur traders, and steamboat men." The main drag was a two-lane road that was bordered with the typical fast-food establishments and hotels, sandy-colored mountains and green vegetation. In modern times, Oacoma is still a stopping-off place, but it is a place for visitors travelling to the Badlands National Park. I stopped on a street where the storefronts looked like a scene out of the wild west and asked someone to take a picture of me riding a metal bull. Once I got back onto the interstate, it took another two hours of driving to reach the Badlands National Park.

I cannot accurately describe what I saw when I reached the Badlands. They looked like the Grand Canyon without a canyon: expansive, beautiful, dusty-looking, colorful, and vast. The 244,000-acre national park is a geological treasure, with rock formations, or "badlands", also a "geological term used to describe soft sedimentary rocks that erode easily." The rock formations, which erode one inch per year, according to the National Park System, provide a look back into time with their "layered sandstones, siltstones, mudstones, clay stones, limestones, volcanic ash, and shale." There are also vast prairie grasslands where animals such as bison and bighorn sheep roam. The park also contains, within its boundaries, archaeological sites and fossils thousands of years old.

Peace reigned in this place. I felt and experienced calmness. I wandered around the grasslands and observed prairie dogs and pronghorn. In the distance, a small patch of towering sunflowers near a sod tower waved in the wind, the towers a remnant of the ancient prairie. I immediately thought of my mom. For her, sunflowers were Dan's way of speaking to her, just as "Grizzly" was Dan's word for me. I snapped a photo and immediately texted it to her. Within minutes, she texted me back with a smile. I got back on the interstate and headed toward the Mount Rushmore National Memorial in the Black Hills National Forest, a 90-minute drive.

I gave Jerry Williams a call. Since I had started this road trip adventure, we had talked every day. Our calls were short, usually about 20 to 30 minutes. We talked about Ohio State University football, and my relationships with women, to which he would reply with a funny reference to a Jerry

Seinfeld episode. I had to laugh because I knew he was right. When I was in Michigan, I had been talking to a lady from California but had decided to put that on hold for now. I was more focused on living life and enjoying the adventure.

"Hey, Darren. What was that?" Jerry asked.

A bunch of bikers passed me by. There were groups of them, bikers on Harleys, with the stereotypical long moustaches and long beards, leather jackets, tattooed arms, girls riding on the backs of their bikes. Biker girls, too. I had seen a sign earlier advertising Sturgis.

"Hey, Jerry," I joked. "Do you think I should go to Sturgis?" Here I was driving a grocery getter, decked out in a blue V-neck t-shirt, shorts, and flip flops, my usual attire. I could not stop laughing.

"Yeah, you should go, Darren. Why not?"

Sturgis is a city in South Dakota and the home of the Sturgis annual motorcycle festival—held in the city and the surrounding Black Hills Forest. The event was originally started in 1938 by riders of the Indian Motorcycle, an American brand manufactured from 1901 to 1951. In its beginnings, the rally focused on tricks and jumps, then later included racing. It grew from a two-day to a ten-day event starting the first Friday in August. This year there was a record 700,000 people in attendance.

"Yeah, I think I'm going to pass this year, Jerry," I said as I drove in the opposite direction taking Highway 16 south.

Most of my conversations with Jerry were spent laughing. They say laughter is the best medicine and our conversations certainly made me feel at peace during these times of uncertainty.

"Hey, Darren. Where are you headed now?"

"I just turned off the interstate. I've always wanted to see Mount Rushmore."

"How far away are you from Colorado?"

"Not sure, Jerry. I was planning on taking I-90 all the way to California. What's in Colorado?"

"I think you should go see Brad," Jerry said.

I had never met Brad, but I had heard of him. Jerry explained that Brad was a vital part of the RSS leadership team, and if I was thinking of joining forces with RSS in the future, I would need to connect with Brad.

"When you meet him, Brad's probably going to ask you about your five-year plan," Jerry said. "He's a different kind of thinker. Good for the team."

Five-year plan? I wasn't even thinking about a few days ahead, other than getting to San Diego.

Jerry explained that Brad had been a successful manager with Vector Marketing, like my mentor Mike Bella. Upon hearing that, I was impressed. Brad must have been a special person to be able to reach that level at Vector.

"Sure, Jerry. I'll go. Just going to stop by Mount Rushmore first."

"Sounds good, Darren. Talk later."

I was nearing the Mount Rushmore National Memorial but planned to cut the visit short, knowing that I would need to take a big left turn and head south. I parked my car near the monument and took a photo of the famous granite rock containing the carved likenesses of the four presidents—George

Washington, Thomas Jefferson, Theodore Roosevelt, and Abraham Lincoln. Now I was off to Colorado, via a highway through the wilderness of Wyoming.

Wyoming is the least populous of the continental states, with a population a little more than one-half million, yet it is filled with some of the most picturesque views of snow-capped mountains in the distance, even in the summertime. I was driving west of the Rocky Mountain chain, but I could still see its beauty from far away. After a while, I started getting hungry when a sign for Chugwater Chili appeared along the roadside, the best chili in Wyoming it said, and I just had to stop. I would grab a bite to eat, have some conversation, then look for a place to stay for the night.

The tiny town of Chugwater, population 800, housed the small brick one-story building with a sign that read, "Chugwater Soda Fountain, Beer – Liquor – Gifts." I walked through the glass door and a bell chimed. An older lady greeted me.

"Wyoming is such a beautiful state," I said with a smile on my face. "I'd like a bowl of your best chili!"

"Oh, It's horrible here."

"The chili?" I asked.

"No, Wyoming. Came out here 39 years ago. Wanted to be a cowgirl. Not what I expected."

I tried to put a smile on her face but, to say the least, I was not successful. The chili, however, was absolutely delicious. It turns out that they make their own chili spices and sell them, too. As the sun was setting, I realized that I had grossly underestimated how remote Wyoming is. In other words, it is not the easiest place to find a hotel. I drove in the pitch darkness until I reached Cheyenne, the largest city in Wyoming, just north of the Colorado border, where I found a place to settle for the night. The next morning I called Brad and we agreed to meet in Denver for lunch.

The drive from Cheyenne to Denver was a straight shot south. With the grasslands to the east and the Rocky Mountains to the west, I felt as if I was in cowboy country. The sky had already grown dark when I had reached Cheyenne the night before, but now in the morning light, I could see the majesty of the Rockies. After entering the state of Colorado, I passed through Fort Collins, one of the larger cities that lined the interstate before reaching Denver. Brad and I decided to meet at one of RSS's locations before having lunch. My first impression of Brad was that he was intelligent, well-spoken, and approachable.

Our meeting was quick. He listened to my "five-year-plan", which was namely to simplify RSS's complex business model. In order for the company to grow in the future, I repeated the same message I had relayed to Scott about creating small, duplicatable mattress shops. Brad liked the idea.

While I believed that connecting with the RSS leadership team would solidify my future with the company a year from now, I also maintained my focus on the present, specifically that I needed to drive through the Rockies while it was still daylight. The city of Denver is called the mile-high city because it is at an elevation of 5,280 feet. Now that I was heading west on I-70, I headed into the foothills of the Rockies reaching even higher elevations. The winding highway was crowded, but I kept with the flow of the racing traffic. In the distance, I could see Mt. Evans at 14,271 feet, which is higher than the more well-known Pikes Peak in Colorado Springs with an elevation of 14,115 feet. Colorado is known for its 14'ers, or mountain peaks that exceed 14,000 feet. In fact, many

Coloradans often describe cities and towns by their elevation. The traffic seemed to subside once I passed the town of Silverthorne adjacent to the Dillon Reservoir, where Highway 9 heads north to Steamboat Springs. I continued travelling west on I-70 driving past the well-known ski resorts, such as Keystone, Breckenridge, and Copper Mountain before stopping at Vail, with a population of 5,000, and an elevation of 8,150 feet.

Nestled in the Rocky Mountains, the Vail Ski resort looks like something out of a travel magazine. Vail village has a European flair to it, with Swiss-style structures bearing colorful waving flags and hanging pots of flowers. I stopped in one of the shops and bought a hat with the Colorado flag—a background of three horizontal stripes, a white stripe flanked by two blue ones—and a large red letter "C" filled with a golden disk in the foreground. Even though it was August, the second warmest month in Colorado, the temperatures were only in the 70's. The feel of the cool, dry mountain air and the views of the picturesque snow-capped mountains made Vail a peaceful place to visit. I continued driving another two hours west through the mountains, stopping near Grand Junction for the night.

The next morning, I crossed into Utah, reaching the place where the tree-lined Rockies meet the red earth and rock of the desert. I was on my way to Arches National Park, near the town of Moab, a place where the Colorado River carves through canyons like a snake in the sand. It was still early that morning when I set off to hike to the Delicate Arch. It did not think it would matter that it was nearly 100 degrees, or that I was only wearing a pair of flip flops. On my head was my Colorado hat and in my pocket a rock with "Dream Big" inscribed onto it. When I decided to go into business, one of my signature lines was, "Dream Big, Work Hard, Always Smile." Yes, I was up for the challenge. I just did not realize that it would be an uphill two-hour hike kind of challenge.

From afar, the red arches of the Delicate Arch looked like sculptures of the desert untouched by nature. During my trek, I came across a one-room cabin built by 69-year-old John Wesley Wolfe, who had left his wife and three of his children, to live in a drier climate due to a leg injury he got in battle during the Civil War. He brought his oldest son with him and together they started a 100-acre ranch. A visit from his daughter, her husband, and their two children eight years later resulted in the building of the cabin. To live in that kind of environment, with six people under one roof, was unbelievable to me.

Near the Wolfe Ranch were massive slabs of rock with Ute Indian petroglyphs of bighorn sheep and native peoples on horseback. The National Park System states that "this rock art was created after the mid-1600s when the native people in this area acquired horses." But many peoples migrated to this area thousands of years before, such as "hunter-gatherers … about 10,000 years ago at the end of an Ice Age." Knowing that people had crossed this place before me made me feel as if I was on a similar path. This was not about me doing a cross-country road trip. It had become more than that. Others had passed through this area, each one with their own story. And, I definitely had my own story. We all have stories.

Eventually, I reached the Delicate Arch. I did a handstand in the middle of it to celebrate, feeling proud that I conquered this hike. Now, I just had to hike back where water and air conditioning would be awaiting me. When I opened the car door, my cell phone was ringing and I had to take the call. It was Scott.

He and Daphene happened to be in Las Vegas. I mentioned that I was about six hours away at Arches National Park. Would I like to meet him and his wife for Thai food around 7 p.m., he asked? They had come to Las Vegas to attend a furniture show and they were meeting with a vendor. Sure, I could make that happen. Going to Vegas would be an excellent way to get to know the couple better.

Chapter Seven

After meeting with the Andrews for dinner, I left the desert oasis of Las Vegas and headed toward California. The meeting had been a good one and a short one. The interstate that runs through southwestern Nevada, I-15, is called the Las Vegas Highway. Lined with red rocks, the highway runs through a desert wonderland of barren, dusty-looking mountains. As I drove through this vast desert dotted with small communities that offered last-chance gambling, I wondered if I would ever see green trees and grass, or even water, again. Some of the areas I passed through had businesses but no residents, like the commercial town called Jean, home of the Jean Sport Aviation Center. Not a soul lives there, but the town has a hotel, a casino, a post office, and an all-female correctional facility. Near the Nevada-California border was the unincorporated community of Primm, formerly called State Line.

Western California's geography, like Nevada, is mountainous desert. Onward I continued with air conditioning blasting, the hot sun beating on the roof of my car. Along the way, I saw a sign for a rattlesnake habitat area and a ghost town before reaching Barstow. Finally, civilization and a Wal-Mart! In the distance were the San Bernardino mountains tracing the horizon, with San Diego just beyond the mountain chain. The highway widened and, with it, the traffic flow increased exponentially. I stayed on I-15 until it flowed into I-5, then headed south toward Encinitas, a beach city north of San Diego, where I had booked a hotel for five days. I had driven across the country in six days covering nearly 3,000 miles!

After doing an online search for a place to live, I connected with a woman who was renting her guestroom. She had a beautiful three-bedroom condo on the intracoastal waterway in Carlsbad. After meeting with her in person, I felt comfortable with her as a roommate. So, I settled in and unpacked my few belongings. I gave Katie a call to tell her I had made it to North County. I met with her and her boyfriend at a juice bar. It felt comforting to see a familiar face.

I also started looking for recovery meetings to attend. By this time, I had maintained my sobriety for seven years, and I wanted it to stay that way. In Jacksonville Beach, I had been regularly attending a private small men's group on Tuesday nights. It was usually the same group of guys. One of those guys, in particular, was named Joe. Now, in the San Diego area, there were hundreds of meetings available on any given night. I was not currently working so I did not have any limitations as to when I could attend. I just picked a meeting and showed up. As soon as I walked into the room, I saw a familiar face! Joe from Jacksonville Beach. I never saw Joe again after that night. Neither did I ever connect with Katie and her boyfriend again but seeing these familiar faces made me realize that my past was somehow connecting me to the present.

At the time, I was not focused on establishing a serious romantic relationship with anyone. Even though my marriage had ended, my plan had always been to return to Jacksonville Beach. Yet I was open to meeting someone who might want to go back with me. When I was in Michigan, I had joined a dating site and connected with a woman who lived in the San Diego area. I called her, we met, and then dated for about a month. It felt good to have companionship again. The two of us had yoga in common, and she told me about a great yoga studio, but, other than that, we did not have enough of a connection for the relationship to last.

The city of Carlsbad was peaceful and I enjoyed living there, but I felt, at times, as if I were living a lie. I was 45 years old and had all of my belongings with me except for a few things I had left in Ohio with my mom. I did not connect with any of my friends on Facebook, and I had deleted my profile on LinkedIn, virtually cutting off all of my past business associates and connections, people who were my acquaintances, friends, and colleagues. For the first time in my life, I felt isolated.

Despite the isolation, my life in California was going smoothly. That is, until my attorney called me with some bad news. He said he could no longer represent me, even though I had just paid him thousands of dollars. I should have seen that coming based upon his behavior at the deposition. He ended the call by telling me the judge had found me in contempt of court, and that I was ordered to go to jail for 60 days! *This was a civil lawsuit, and yet I needed to go to jail?* I could not believe it. Apparently, someone reported to the court that I attended RSS's first national sales meeting. That was untrue. I had never attended. I knew and respected the rules of the court. I knew what I was and what I was not permitted to do. I had not broken any of the rules.

A couple of days after I received the phone call from my ex-attorney, there was a knock on the door and a police officer on the other side. My heart started racing. Why was he here? Was he going to haul me off to jail? The officer, who was holding an envelope in his hand, asked if my landlord was home. Apparently, she was being served with divorce papers. Even though the officer had not come for me, I was still scared as well as scarred from the experience. Terrified, in fact. The longer I stayed in Carlsbad, the more I felt as if I was secretly hiding something, even though I had nothing to hide. Psychologically and emotionally, all of this drama was wearing on me. It was honesty that kept me sober. I was being honest, and I wanted and needed to stay sober. But all of this drama made me feel as if I was keeping secrets. I paid my landlord the October rent and sent some money to Chloe.

I then left California for Florida. Ironically, my plan was to report to jail so I could finally be free. I called my mom and told her what I was planning to do. She was frustrated. But, before I could react, another call came in and I ended the call with Mom in order to take it. It was Jerry. I picked up the call but did not say a word. I was too emotionally spent to say anything.

"Hey, Darren," my friend's familiar voice said. "Where are you? I think we have a solution for you. How close are you to Tucson?" I had already made it to the Arizona-New Mexico border, so I was about a two-hour drive away.

One of RSS's dealers, Tucson Furniture Direct, Jerry explained, had $150,000 in inventory that needed to be sold. Could I help?

"I'm supposed to go to jail, Jerry. I just can't do it. Sorry."

I do not remember Jerry's reply verbatim, but it was something along the lines of him and Scott taking care of everything if I could help in Tucson. I listened to his words and felt reassured, as if I could trust his judgment. So, I turned the car around and headed to Tucson.

The Tucson store, once a bus depot, was located at 1100 Plumber Avenue, where Plumber intersected with 22nd Street. This detail probably would not be significant to most people, but it was to me. November 22, or 11/22, was the date I became sober. So, for me, the address of the Tucson store was not a coincidence. Seeing Joe at the recovery meeting in Carlsbad was not a coincidence. Nor were the Grizzly encounters on my road trip across America coincidences. My life story had less to do with coincidences, I believe, and more to do with connections. Every time something like this happened, I felt as if God was saying, "Darren, this is where you're supposed to be."

The owner of the store, a retired master sergeant in the Air Force, had spent his days sitting at his desk, letting his salespeople run the store for him. Obviously, this approach had not been working. So, I built a rapport with him. We sat together and I explained why establishing a simple business model was important to the success of his business. Within six weeks, all of the inventory had been sold. In fact, the Tucson store became one of the top locations in the country. It felt good to help in this manner, even with no guarantees in return. I felt as if I had righted a ship. For the next three months, I helped him run the store, and held informal training sessions for the employees and others interested in getting into the business at the store.

I did not spend all of my time working in Arizona, however. The store owner and I became good friends. We even joined a bowling league together. Arizona was also a land of beauty with plenty of outdoor activities. One of my favorite places to go was Mount Lemmon, elevation 9,159 feet. About 40 miles northeast of Tucson in the Santa Catalina Mountains, Mount Lemmon, with its tree-covered mountains, canyons, waterfalls, and rock formations, was also a popular skiing and hiking destination. One afternoon, after I had hiked to the summit alone, I saw that the ski lift was running but that no one had been riding in it. In fact, nobody had been hiking that day either, which was strange. What was even more strange was who, or rather, what approaching on the lift. A giant stuffed Grizzly bear was enjoying a ride up the mountain, sitting snuggly on one of the seats. This could not have been a coincidence because I no longer believed in coincidences! The Grizzly bear appearances were an assurance that my brother Dan was still here with me, guiding me, supporting me, and letting me know that everything was going to be okay.

Back in town while I was assisting at the Tucson store one day, a man dressed in scrubs came into the store. We started talking, as I usually did with all of the customers. He happened to mention that he worked for Dr. Schroeder. I was amazed because Dr. Schroeder was the neurosurgeon who had operated on me when I was a teen during the short period of time when I was living with my dad in Arizona. I was amazed that the good doctor was still doing surgeries 30 years later! What were the chances that I would make this connection if it were not to be for some reason? Slim to none.

I was 17 years old when I was living with my dad, an army commander at Fort Huachuca. We lived in Sierra Vista, Arizona, close to the U.S.-Mexican border. Moving there was a gift, a gift of second chances. I had dropped out of school at age 16 in Ohio and moved in with my dad. In Ohio, I had not been a good student. I was always late to school. I could not focus and I did not know how to study. I struggled with the routine of school life. Moving to Arizona was an opportunity to set things right and get my life back in order. I enrolled in high school again. I tried out for the basketball team and joined the Junior ROTC. But it was hard to give up the party lifestyle. I was smoking cigarettes and kept on partying and drinking. Now, the military guys only had to be 18 to drink. So, with the haircut and the Junior ROTC uniform, I definitely looked the part. But I got caught one night in the women's barracks on base and the Sergeant Major picked me up and brought me home to my dad because I was so intoxicated. I can honestly say that Dad was not too happy about that.

But living in Arizona was not altogether a negative experience for me. One of my major accomplishments was keeping a running schedule. I ran five miles every day. One afternoon after school, I was jogging on Highway 92. I was wearing white sweatpants and a white tee shirt in the afternoon sun, running at a good pace and feeling pretty good. The next thing I knew I was lying flat on my back. A cyclist had struck me from behind and toppled on me, bike and all. My head was throbbing and I could not move. I was taken to the ER on the military base then sent home.

That night, at Dad's house, I started coughing up blood. Pressure was building inside of my head and the pain had become excruciating. I became comatose and had to be life-flighted to the hospital. My skull had been fractured, which caused a blood clot to form on my brain. The ER had misdiagnosed me yet still here I was, given a second chance to live.

My prognosis was not good. I had to undergo neurosurgery. The six-hour surgery was intense, though obviously I was asleep during all of it. My mother could not fly to Arizona to be by my side because she was pregnant with my brother John at the time. After the surgery, Dr. Schroeder informed my parents that I might experience learning disabilities. All I remember after the operation is waking up and placing my hand on my head. Half of my hair had been shaved! The bumps from the staples on my skin felt like train tracks. When the doctor came into the room to check on me, he did not have a smile on his face. He just said that I would not be able to move the right side of my face or play sports anymore. I was still coming out of it, half-listening to what he said but did not believe a word of it. Instead, I felt determined to prove him wrong. Once I got back home, my dad's mom flew from Ohio to Arizona to take care of me. She cooked for me. Made sure I had clean clothes. It was a blessing, to be sure, but, at the time, I felt like she was treating me like a child. She left Arizona upset and I never saw her again. She passed away a year later. I regretted my behavior but there was nothing I could do to change the past. Instead, I focused on the present, improving as a student, doing well in school, and playing sports again.

Yes, Arizona was the place where I had been given second chances, and it was also the place where I overcame my first obstacle. Here I was again, thirty years later, being given a second chance yet again and facing yet another obstacle. I was now an employee of a furniture store, which was, in a way, a potential steppingstone to a future role with RSS leadership. For an additional three months, I stayed in Tucson helping out at the store and holding informal training sessions for those who might be interested in getting into the business.

During my stay in Arizona, Scott was also personally helping me as a friend, not as a business partner, by paying the rent on my apartment. At one point, his wife Daphene and her sister flew in from South Carolina for a visit. They stayed at the apartment for a week, which, at first felt awkward because

I am an introvert and need space to recharge. But I always believed in going with the flow. The three of us had dinner together and we went hiking. I was still technically being sued by Scott, but the couple trusted me. Daphene's visit solidified that trust. Scott's son, Aaron, had also expressed interest in becoming a part of the family business. Later that year, Aaron came to Tucson to learn the business. The plan was that we would both go to southern California in January where I would help him open his own store.

But not before we attended the 45th Fiesta Bowl in Phoenix. On New Year's Day 2016, Ohio State would be playing Notre Dame. These two teams had not played against each other since Fiesta Bowl 2006. As a diehard Ohio State Buckeyes fan, there was no way I could not attend this game. I bought tickets for Aaron and me. The plan was to drive to Phoenix on New Year's Eve, where I would meet with some old fraternity buddies, then we would go to the game on New Year's Day. Unfortunately, Aaron got sick, so I travelled to Phoenix by myself. My fraternity brothers did not show up at the bar (which might not have been a good idea anyway) where we were supposed to meet. I looked for a recovery group on my phone and found one that was hosting a New Year's Eve event. One of the people at the meeting invited me to join the others for game night at his house. I went and had a great time but I did not stay out late because the football game was at 11 a.m. the next day.

The next morning, I got up early and drove to the University of Phoenix Stadium in Glendale. It was packed with 80,000 screaming fans. In the first quarter, we led by 14 points, with two touchdowns, one by Ezekiel Elliot, who now plays for Dallas, and the other by Michael Thomas, who now plays for New Orleans. Notre Dame tried to catch up, with Josh Adams, who now plays for the New York Jets, scoring a three-yard touchdown. But Ezekiel Elliot scored two more touchdowns, getting us ahead with a score of 14-28 by half-time.

I was so ramped up because the Buckeyes had such an advantage going into the second half. But anything can happen during the final minutes of a football game. Still, I was reeling. We were annihilating The Fighting Irish. During half-time, as I made my way through the crowd of indistinguishable faces, my stomach dropped. Standing in front of me was my first wife, Melanie. She was with her daughter and her daughter's husband, and with some guy I have never seen. "Darren. Oh my God. How are you?" she smiled and gave me a hug. I was instantly transported back in time to the day I had met her in Columbus, Ohio, when I had been working for PMD. She had made an appointment to buy a mattress. She was so beautiful that I asked her out on the spot.

We spoke briefly, mostly small talk. I could barely hear her voice over the roaring crowd. There had never been any animosity between the two of us. We both had made mistakes. It just was not meant to be. With half-time almost over, we parted ways and I took my seat waiting for the second half to begin. This half was even better than the first, the highlight being Ezekiel Elliot's 42-yard touchdown run in the third quarter. The Buckeyes topped the score with Sean Nuernberger's three 30-yard plus field goal kicks in the fourth quarter. The Buckeyes were victorious. My team had won!

On the drive back to Tucson, I thought about the chance encounter with Melanie at the OSU football game in Phoenix. *What were the chances of that happening?* It made me think about the forces in this life, and how some people are drawn to us at just the right time to teach us a lesson. But I was not quite sure what that lesson was at the time.

By the time I got back to Tucson, Aaron was already packed and ready to go to California. Obviously, he was feeling better, so we headed out the next day. The drive took about six hours. He led the way in his pick-up truck, and I followed in the Denali. I had already driven to California several times but would never tire from the ride. There is something about travelling through the desert amidst the rock formations, the colors and the sand, and then, upon crossing the California state line, seeing the majestic mountains reveal themselves as a pathway to the sea, signifying yet another new beginning. We settled in Oceanside, renting a beautiful two-bedroom condo on Pacific Way near the marina. The store location, a 1,500 square foot warehouse on the 101 near Camp Pendleton, was only a five-minute walk, or two-minute drive, from the condo. Here I was at age 45 with a roommate twenty years my junior. Yet, despite the age difference, I felt as if we were compadres ready to take on a new journey, with me guiding him along the way.

Once I settled back into California life, I thought about Chloe. We still had not finalized our divorce. Running into Melanie, my first wife, was an epiphany. I realized that I had been making the same mistakes in my relationships, just with different people. Before I could think about it any further, I picked up my cell phone and called Chloe. She picked up right away. Would you like to fly out to California, honey, I asked her? Do you think we could make things work? I knew it would be a longshot because I now lived on the opposite coast 3,000 miles away unable to come home for fear of being sent to jail. Would Chloe really want to make things work?

Yes, she answered. Absolutely. Let's try again.

Chapter Eight

The name BoxDrop® Mattress & Furniture Direct, a franchise under the parent company RSS, was coined by CEO Scott Andrew sometime during the spring of 2015. At that time, the catchy brand name was not yet being used by its 18 diverse mattress dealers. After the injunction, when I suggested to my Mattress Direct dealers that they team with RSS, RSS grew to approximately 45 stores. Aaron's store in Oceanside, however, was the first official BoxDrop® location.

Aaron was an intelligent young man, genuine and thoughtful. A logical and analytical thinker, he had not been satisfied with being an EMT after his time in the military. Only one week after opening the BoxDrop® Oceanside location, Aaron quickly caught on. Soon after the store opened, I had planned to meet with Scott and Daphene, as well as Jerry Williams, at the furniture market in Las Vegas. But the day before I was supposed to leave on the trip, my car had been stolen. Aaron and I lived in a gated community; in fact, there were double gates! I always parked my car in the same space, and I always left a well-hidden spare key in the car just in case I forgot mine. I filed a police report and, the next day, took a cab to the airport. Once I got to Las Vegas, I found out Jerry was going to play in a celebrity poker tournament for autism. I knew nothing about poker, but I knew I had to enter the competition. Jerry gave me a few poker tips and that was that. There were a couple hundred people playing and it felt good being a part of the competition, connecting with people, having some laughs. As the tournament continued into the night, I found myself at the final table. Just when I was about to play my hand, my phone started buzzing in my jacket pocket. It was a California number. I picked up the call and found myself talking to the Oceanside police who said they found my car stripped to the frame just a few miles away from the condo. My golf clubs were missing, too. I told the cops I was out of town and thanked them for their help. Then, I played my hand, finishing eighth, winning some cash prizes.

The furniture market was held at the World Market Center in Las Vegas, which had 1,000 or so elaborately decorated showrooms throughout six different buildings. We followed a regimented schedule of back-to-back 90-minute appointments from 9 a.m. to 5 p.m. with current and potential vendors, and we stuck to that schedule like clockwork. We looked at everything from pillows to mattress protectors, adjustable bases, memory mattresses, high-end mattresses, anything new and improved in the industry. If we got a good word-of-mouth referral, we would check out that vendor, too. Our goal was to always make sure we had enough inventory for our supply chain. We wanted not only to serve our dealers, who were our customers, but also the public, our dealers' customers. At lunch time, the vendors provided elaborate and sumptuous fare, such as crab legs, sushi, and Prime Rib. At night, the vendors took us out to dinner at five-star restaurants, treating us as if we were royalty.

In July 2015, when I had been temporarily staying in Bellaire, Michigan, I had flown to Tucson to meet with Scott, Daphene, and Jerry, after having just met the couple at their home in South Carolina and reconnecting with my old friend Jerry Williams in Columbus. In Tucson, the four of us met with Kevin Mitchell, a national wholesale furniture accounts vendor, who was also a good friend. We spent two days putting together a nine-mattress line-up to show at RSS's national conference that would take place in August 2016. Each mattress served as a price point to ensure that customers could purchase a mattress that would fit into their budget. In addition to the nine, we selected an additional 20 mattresses. We wanted our dealers to feel as if they had a choice in their mattress selection. After our meeting, I flew back to Michigan, finished staining my parents' cabin, then headed west to California.

I hosted my first training in Denver, Colorado, in February 2016. About 40 people attended the training, most of them RSS leadership. There, I taught them what I had written in my playbook: how to create a simple, duplicatable business model and how to ensure success with this model using the right recruiting techniques. By this time, I already had 16 years of experience as a trainer under my belt, so training others felt second nature to me. For the course, I also wrote the first BoxDrop® training manual. The event was so successful that I hosted additional training sessions in other large metropolitan areas, such as San Diego and Atlanta that year.

In February, Chloe flew to California for a visit. It felt good to see her again. We travelled from Oceanside to San Diego on the Amtrak Pacific Surfliner. There, we walked the beach and the pier at Seal Beach, strolled through Balboa Park, visiting the museums, observing the architecture, and enjoying the gardens, before continuing south to visit La Jolla. We had not seen each other in quite a while but I felt as if the future of our relationship looked promising. Every month, for the next several months, she flew to California for a long weekend. One time we rented an Airbnb in Delmar and took a trip to Crystal Cove State Park, with its cliffed beaches, meandering trails, coves, and tide pools. Another time, we travelled to L.A., went to a comedy club, and visited Hollywood and Beverly Hills. Chloe adored flowers so I took her to The Flower Fields in Carlsbad, a 50-acre field of ranunculus flowers, which en masse looked like delicate, small roses.

Long distance relationships, no matter how much you love a person, can be difficult to maintain, all the more so when you are trying to work on your relationship from afar. When we were together, it felt like an escape from our real-world troubles. We laughed, loved, and enjoyed each other's company. But, when I dropped Chloe off at the airport, I felt an aching and a sadness inside. I would kiss her goodbye, give her a hug, and watch her walk through security unsure when or if I would see her again. Then, I would wait next to the car in the parking lot and watch her plane take off, unsure if it was even her plane. As I drove home, it always felt like a piece of me was missing, like my arm had been ripped off or my heart had a hole drilled into it. Her parting always reminded me that I could not go back to Jacksonville Beach.

Aaron spent long days in the showroom. He would come home and relax, preferring to spend his time alone. My social calendar, however, seemed as if it was booked weeks in advance. If I was not travelling with Chloe, I was attending a birthday party or cookout. I made many friends from my recovery meetings and had also reconnected with my network of friends from when I lived in Carlsbad. I did yoga and had friends in the yoga community and I also met with the Ohio State alumni, especially the football fans. I also had a close friend named Matt with whom I travelled throughout southern California. We visited Tony Robbins' 10,000-square foot castle in DelMar, as well as the horse racetrack there.

I was Aaron's business mentor and guide, but I also had a personal mentor as well, which was an integral part of my recovery. David was in his seventies. His career with the Forest Service had been extensive. He began as a Landscape Architect, was a District Ranger for the Stanislaus and Coronado Forests, became the Monterey District Ranger on the Los Padres National Forest, an Assistant Regional Director of Recreation National Forests and Grasslands in Arizona, New Mexico, Oklahoma, and Texas, and ended his work with the Forest Service as a National Program Director at the Washington office. We met at Buddy Todd Park in Oceanside. As I pulled into the entrance, I was greeted at by none other than a giant, wooden carving of a Grizzly bear standing on its hind legs. All along this journey, I felt as if my younger brother Dan had been by my side. It was like he kept sending me messages that everything was going to be alright. I was told that the carving had been hit by lightning just two weeks before, but it did not look like it was damaged. I was looking at the carving, thinking about my younger brother when David arrived. I could not help telling him about my brother Dan and the Grizzly encounters I had had since coming from Michigan. David was congenial and friendly. He was also a good listener as I had a lot of things to say. During the course of our conversation, he recommended two books: *The Surrender Experiment* by Michael Singer and *The Magic* by Robin Burn. One is a daily practice for 30 days and the other is the true story of Mike Singer and his journey of surrendering. I realized that in order to grow, I needed to surrender.

That meant saying "yes" when I wanted to say "no." One of those occasions happened to be accepting an invitation to a camping trip at Palomar Mountain State Park, about an hour west of Oceanside. My friend Matt had invited me to go with him. My first instinct was to say something like, "No way. I don't want to spend a weekend camping with a bunch of dudes." Instead, I said "yes" and spent an extended weekend with 13 guys who were also in recovery. The irony was that Matt, at the last minute, could not attend so I was on my own. I knew nothing about camping. I loaded a queen-sized mattress from the store into the back of my car and headed west. The mountains were green, filled with the scent of pine trees, fir trees, and cedar trees. The remote campsite was near a pristine lake, which was good for trout fishing. The leaders of this annual expedition, Terry and Johnny, had been hosting this trip for the past 22 years. I was impressed.

Every day, for the next four days, we attended three meetings, one for each of the 12 recovery steps. It felt good to be a part of something. Everybody had a job to do. My task was making coffee in the morning. That might seem like a simple job, but it was not as easy as it sounds. I had to get up early and make coffee on the fire in six different coffee pots, the old school kind that did not make a lot of cups. All 14 of us were in recovery and we all needed at least two to three cups in the morning. Others were in charge of cooking, cleaning up, or making a fire. On the first night, as I was getting settled into my tent, the earth started shaking violently. It felt as if I was going to be swallowed whole. The tremor lasted all of 15 seconds, but it was certainly the topic of conversation over coffee the next morning. Welcome to camping in California!

The hours passed quickly. By the time we cleaned up our

makeshift outdoor kitchen after breakfast, it was almost time to start making lunch. Between lunch and dinner was the time when we hiked, played cornhole, or went trout fishing. At night we would hang out by the campfire and talk. One day, the fog rolled in and we played cornhole in the fog. Here, in nature, everything was still and quiet. We slept outdoors. The air was fresh, and the forest sounds were calming. We woke up in the morning feeling exhilarated. Then, it was time to make the coffee again.

Recovering from alcoholism involves a succession of twelve steps practiced throughout a lifetime. When I adopted those principles into my own life, it brought me a significant amount of peace, joy and serenity. As I went through the process of becoming sober, I felt as if I was continually changing. Recovery is a process of discovery, like peeling an onion and finding the hidden layers beneath. Sometimes we do not realize what we need to do to recover until it becomes uncovered and revealed.

Throughout recovery, one of the steps involves making a list of the people we have harmed as well as the people we need to forgive. The next step is to make amends with both. I was able to write my list but was not sure how to make amends, so I just left that part to God.

Michigan fans (yes, each and every Wolverines fan) was on my list. I hate to admit it but I used to hate Michigan Wolverines' fans. In fact, I could not even say the word "Michigan." The rivalry between our two college football teams was so intense that it was obviously not very healthy. After all, we are all people created by God in His image. But, for me, a die-hard Ohio State Buckeyes fan, I had to learn how to forgive Michigan Wolverines' fans.

When the guys found out I was an Ohio State Buckeye, they jokingly warned me about another guy, Wes, who would be joining us at the campout later that night. It turns out that Wes was a die-hard Wolverine's fan! (Californians are not big on college football, but they do talk football. You can tell a lot about a man by which football team he supports.) The guys started heckling me about the potential cornhole game between the Buckeyes and the Wolverines. The good thing is that I had already worked out my anger against Wolverine fans long ago. When Wes arrived at the campsite, we were introduced and all went well. He was a great guy and we got along. Now as we all sat around the campfire that night, Wes mentioned that today was the 7th anniversary of his sobriety. Terry and Johnny said they were sorry but they did not have a coin to give him. None of the other guys had a coin either, let alone a 7th year anniversary coin. I remembered that I had put my 7th year coin in my wallet. Now, I had never have carried a coin with me, whether it was a 1st, 2nd, 3rd year, and so on. I just never did. I was also on a camping trip and should have stowed my wallet in the car, but I had my wallet with me. In that wallet was my 7th anniversary coin that I had received about six months ago. What were the chances of that happening? Slim to none. I reached into my wallet, pulled out the coin, and gave it to Wes. He was surprised yet thankful. I realized that the Lord works in mysterious ways. I did not know how to make amends. But the Lord did and He showed me how!

With the camping trip over, I felt a bit of a letdown. But it was time to leave the mountains and get back to city living. Several days after my return, it was Mother's Day, so I gave Mom a call. She said she wanted me to fly to Michigan to spend the Fourth of July with the family. It had been nearly a year since I had seen her, Pops, and John, and, of course,

I wanted to go. Not only that, Fourth of July is one of those family holidays that you do not skip. It is as important as Christmas. It felt like I had just been at the cabin. The year had gone by quickly, and so much had happened. I had left my home, my business, and my marriage and was now trying to rebuild my marriage and my future life. I had also driven across the country from Florida to Michigan, from Michigan to California, from California to Arizona and back to California again. I had met new and interesting people, visited places I had never seen, some of which most do not know even exist, and increased my network a hundred-fold, or more. Not to mention trying to solidify a foundation with RSS, a company that I might or might not be part owner of in the future. I had put my simple business model into action expecting nothing in return, still always hoping for the best.

The conversation between Mom and me shifted, and we started talking about Dan. The tears started flowing and I could no longer talk. Mom was crying, too. I pulled off of the highway and parked the car. Still talking to Mom, I hiked down one of the winding paths that led to the ocean. The cliffs at Carlsbad were a place I often visited for solace and consolation. From above, I could see the line in the sky where the cold, turbulent waters meet the horizon, and the white waves crash upon the rock. The pathway looked as if it had been carved by an ancient raging river that had been lost in time. I looked down at the earthen-colored rock and saw the name "Dan" carved into it. There were no other carvings, no other etchings, no graffiti, just the name Dan. What were the chances of seeing the name Dan when Mom and I were missing him so much? Hadn't he been sending me signs of his presence all along? He had been, and that was what he was trying to tell me.

By June, I sensed that Aaron was getting frustrated. It is difficult being an entrepreneur. When you first start a business, you are working a lot of hours and you are not making a lot of money. The store he was running, however, was a company location, so the company paid for everything. In his case, the company happened to be his family. At times, it seemed as if he wanted to express his doubts or frustrations, but it felt awkward because I was hoping to do business with his family. I tried to stay as neutral as possible. Around that time, a false online smear campaign had been launched against me. Aaron had done an internet search on my name and found out that I did not look as good online as I did in person. In any event, his findings, though untrue, probably did not increase his confidence in me as his mentor. Aaron started packing one day and he told me he was leaving. I did not try to stop him. I was okay with his decision. I knew that he was on his own life path and I fully supported him. Once he left, people were clamoring to take over the Oceanside location. One of my friends, Ben Owen, took over the store and, later on, he opened up several more locations.

With the Fourth of July holiday soon approaching, I booked a flight to Michigan. I called Chloe hoping that she would join me. Would she like to meet me in Michigan this month for the holiday? We could stay at the cabin, enjoy the lakes, light fireworks, visit with the family? Her answer came as a surprise even though I knew that our paths had been diverging ever since I left Florida. She did not let me down gently, and I cannot say that her answer did not hurt, but I realized how hard it must have been for her not knowing when I would return to Florida. After all, neither did I.

Chapter Nine

On the fifth of July I flew back to California so I could pick up my best friend Valter from the airport. He is from Jacksonville Beach and is someone who has always had my back, no matter what. Exactly two months apart in age, we are also exactly two months apart in sobriety.

For eight days we travelled up and down the southern California coast. We visited Oceanside's outdoor market with its hundreds of vendors, and Ruby's Diner, a 50's-themed restaurant at Oceanside Pier. Before Valter decided to travel to California, I had already arranged a date with a Californian woman so he came along with us. The three of us went kayaking at Oceanside Harbor. Yes, the three of us! A military trainer, my date was able to get us onto the Marine base at Camp Pendleton. We spent the afternoon walking along the pristine beach at the base and eating lunch at a tiki hut.

After Valter flew back to Florida, it was not long until William moved in. He was in his twenties and had already been a part of my California recovery network for a while. A recovering alcoholic, William had been living in a sober living facility, but the environment was not exactly supportive of a sober lifestyle. I knew that I would not be staying in California much longer, but I wanted to offer him at least a temporary place to stay.

When August came, it was time to travel to Las Vegas once again but not for the furniture market. I would be attending my first RSS national conference. Even though the one-year anniversary of the injunction had passed, my case was still being negotiated in the Florida courts. When my attorney had resigned last year, Jerry and Scott had hired another to represent me. The new attorney assured me that it was perfectly legal for me to attend the conference.

When I arrived in Las Vegas, the air was dry and hot. Like triple digits hot. There is no way to prepare for this kind of heat. One must just endure it. I hailed a cab from the airport to Harrah's Resort. The resort's iconic exterior glittered with rows of flickering lights. Massive starlit purple spheres topped with stars and the name "Harrah's'" marking each entryway made the resort hard to miss. I tipped the cabbie and checked in, then made my way to the cocktail meet and greet. I was familiar with some of the people in attendance but not all of them. The small group of 40 attendees was a combination of previous Mattress Direct dealers and former PMD business colleagues—people who knew me well. Yet there were others who saw me as a stranger or even as a competitor. I met George Varn, the RSS National Training Coordinator, who later became a lifelong friend. He was a pillar of the company and had been instrumental in welcoming and transitioning the Mattress Direct dealers into RSS. George had once owned a store location. When he became a corporate leader, his wife Sandy took over the business. My first meeting with the couple was warm, and I felt it had gone well.

The next morning, everyone met in the ballroom for the opening address and large group session. In the afternoon, we attended smaller break-out sessions. I gave a presentation on how to run a small mattress business, which felt a bit awkward. Not because I was not comfortable with presenting. I had been doing that for nearly two decades. It was because, at that time, RSS leadership had not announced that I might be joining the company in the future. So, for those who saw me as a competitor or did not know who I was, it might have seemed confusing as to why I was at the conference, let alone giving a presentation.

That night one of our vendors treated the leadership team as well as the coaches, leaders, managers, and top dealers to a special night out, which included tickets to ride the High Roller at the LINQ. At 550 feet, the High Roller is one of the world's largest Ferris wheels. The slow-moving wheel lined with pods offers spectacular views of the Las Vegas night sky, with the bright city lights against a backdrop of black mountains. The RSS leadership team had reserved the bar car, a large circular open bar with room enough to stand up and mingle. I am afraid of heights, so I cannot say I was enthusiastic about going on the ride. Imagine. I am a recovering alcoholic, afraid of heights, and locked in an open bar car for 30 minutes, rising to and descending from 550 feet, and everyone around me is drinking.

The next morning, we woke early and took the dealers to the furniture market, which had been opened for us exclusively. The focus was on mattresses, and, of course, the nine-mattress line-up that Scott, Daphene, Jerry, and I had created the year before when we met in Tucson. That evening Jerry Williams and I took out a handful of guys to dinner, and to Caesar's Palace pool, with its Romanesque structures and décor, for a swim. Some of the guys had been friends of mine from Mattress Direct. The others were RSS guys, people with whom I was still forging a relationship. It felt like two separate football teams trying to form a new team with a new quarterback. I was no longer in charge anymore. I now knew what it felt like to surrender and it felt strange. I was only a guy on the team, although I was not technically on the team just yet.

All in all, for me, the conference was bittersweet. Yes, I had connected with people whom I had not seen for a long while, people who had been like brothers to me. I was also developing relationships with new people, like Brad Loy and George Varn, as well as Scott and his wife, Daphene. It felt natural and comfortable to be there, and I was fortunate and grateful for the chance to build new relationships, but, still, I did not feel as if I was 100 percent in. I did not have a title or a role. I was just sharing the community vision and bringing people together.

Once I returned to California, I continued meeting with David, my sponsor in recovery. An avid hiker, he arranged a trip for us to explore the wilderness trails at Mount San Jacinto State Park. With the vast number of years he had spent working for the Forest Service, I could not have been in better hands! Together, we rode the Palm Springs Aerial Tramway to Mountain Station, hiked past the ranger station to Round Valley, reaching an elevation of 9,100 feet. The five-mile hike forced me to tackle my fear of heights as I looked down at the massive boulders that lined the mountains. It was not an easy hike, but I had already been used to mountain hiking from my experience at Arches National Park in Utah as well as various mountain hikes I did in California. Once we reached the summit, the views were incredible. We were surrounded by purple, pine-laden mountains in the background touching the crisp, blue sky. From our vantage point, Palm Springs and the desert was to the east. Surrounded by high peaks, we stopped for a while to meditate before looping back to the tram. As we descended the trail, David and I started talking. He asked me how I envisioned my life within the next five years. I did not have to think about my answers. I just spoke from my heart.

David's energy was all-encompassing. He was a very peaceful man. I remember the day I met him. Actually, he just showed up in my life. We had bumped into each other as I was leaving a recovery meeting. I had never seen the man before. He just looked at me and said, "You need to work on some commitment issues." After that, we started meeting regularly at Buddy Todd Park in Oceanside, working through the twelve steps and developing a strong friendship over time. It was David who helped me make the major shifts that I needed to at that time in my life.

At the end of August, I flew to Columbus. College football season was starting, and I wanted to attend the opening game. Jerry Williams and his family had been doing the same tailgate party for the past 20 years, so I hung out with him, met his parents and his aunt and uncle. I stayed another week to attend the second home game and met my brother at The Ugly Mug, a bar near our family's home in Canal Winchester, after the game. My brother had been drinking, I was sober, and we both got up on stage and started singing karaoke. It felt good to be home.

When I returned to California, I realized there was no reason for me to stay any longer. The Oceanside store was doing well and I could fly to do the training sessions from any location. And, with college football season underway, Ohio was calling me home. William was also thinking about heading to Tennessee. So, the two of us decided to set out on the road together. I had already had the experience of driving to California on my own, so I was excited and grateful to share this journey with another person.

We decided to take the scenic route and headed north, first stopping at Calico & Ghost Town Railroad in Buena Park, California, on a whim. Afterwards, we continued west on I-40, traveling through hundreds of miles of desert. We meandered through Kitbab National Forest in northern Arizona, reaching the Northern Rim of the Grand Canyon. As a young kid, I had travelled to the Grand Canyon, but I had never seen this part of it. Here, it was isolated. We saw elk and we saw deer. We spent several hours exploring this beautiful geological formation before heading north into Utah.

By now, it was time to look for a hotel for the night, but everything had been booked. As the night grew darker and the road lonelier, I could feel the driver's side of the car running low. I did not say anything to William, but I imagined he had figured out for himself that we had a flat! When we finally did find a place to stop for the night, we pulled into the parking lot. By now the tire had collapsed to the rim. Next to the hotel, there was conveniently a tire shop that would be opening in the morning. Thank you, God! It was one of those synchronistic moments. Everything was going to work out!

The next day, feeling rested, we had the tire replaced then continued to Arches National Park. Arches had been one of my favorite places and I wanted to share it with William. This time, however, I did not hike in flip flops! From there, we continued west into the Rockies. We stopped in Aspen, Colorado. It was the end of September and the Aspen trees had just started turning gold. The views of the snow-topped purple mountains amidst the yellow leaves bordered by green grasses looked like scenic paintings. From there, it was full steam ahead to Ohio.

Once we arrived in Dublin, we rented a two-bedroom apartment. William had decided to stay in Ohio and offered to pay the rent, reciprocating our arrangement in California. We got there just in time for the next OSU football game. Valter flew in for the game, so we all went to Jerry's tailgate party, my brother and his girlfriend tagging along, then on to the stadium for the game. A good friend of mine, Steve Jones, who had worked with me at Carolina Bedding and Mattress by Appointment, was living in Kentucky at the time and also drove up to see the game. I even managed to get him to wear OSU garb! I was hoping to bring Steve onto the RSS team as well, so the next day, I brought him into the home office and introduced him to everybody. By now, I was feeling more comfortable, like I was moving in the right direction. I knew that my legal battle was also coming to an end soon and that eventually I could make my way back to Jacksonville Beach.

In October, my divorce was finalized. That chapter of my life had now ended. Even though I knew that Chloe's and my relationship was over long ago, there was just something psychologically appealing about having closure. I could start fresh and anew, not just in my personal life, but in all aspects of my life. In October, RSS leadership invited me to their leadership trip. Twelve of us went on a two-day hunting trip in Corsicana, Texas. We stayed in primitive cabins on a 3,000-acre ranch and spent our time hunting wild boar. Wild boar hunting is not easy. They are wild and dangerous animals, large, muscular, furry creatures with horns that could kill a person in an instant. There was something about fearing for your life together that created a bond between all of us.

Although the trip lasted only two days, it was apparent that the two teams were successfully merging into one.

By the time I returned to Ohio, I was already psyched about the upcoming Ohio State-Nebraska game. Both teams were ranked, it was a night game, and I had two tickets. I had been going to OSU college football games since I was seven years old, but my mom had never even been to a game. I called and asked her if she wanted to go. “Don’t you have anyone you want to take?” she asked me. I assured her that I wanted her to accompany me. We lived on opposite sides of town, and I certainly did not want my mom to drive by herself. She was still recovering from a stroke and was not as mobile as she used to be. I am the kind of fan that gets to a game early and leaves late. I also never miss a minute. So, I picked up Mom in the afternoon and we made a day of it. The crowds that attended the OSU games were lively and massive. There were usually 100,000 fans attending a game on any given day, in addition to another 100,000 who were tailgating. Due to the crowds, we had to park far away and had to walk quite a while to get to the stadium. I held Mom’s hand, feeling as if we were on an adventure. Our seats were in C Deck in the rafters. The climb was challenging but we made it. We enjoyed the first half of the game, but midway through the third quarter, Mom turned to me and said, “Darren we need to go home.” I immediately took her hand working our way through the crowd, not caring that the game was still in play. In fact, I would say that was the best football game I have ever attended. It was not about the game, just about the experience of being with Mom.

I stayed in Ohio for two more months, long enough to see the final Ohio State-Michigan game. Throughout this time, I continued hosting the training sessions, which were also informally known as “Darren’s training.” They were officially

BoxDrop® training sessions, however. I also continued helping new dealers set up their locations whenever I could. But I was ready to move from Ohio. I picked New Orleans as my next destination. There were no BoxDrop® locations there. I just felt it would be a good place to establish myself and recruit dealers.

By car, the trip to New Orleans would be a good 1,000 miles. This time I did not plan to stop along the way, however. As I was driving toward The Big Easy, I called a realtor to help me find a place to stay. New Orleans is known for its nightlife and the realtor was telling me about all the great bars and clubs in the area until I told her that I was in recovery. "In that case," she said, "let's first meet at a recovery meeting before we find you a place to stay." It turns out that she was in recovery as well. Once again, God kept putting the right people in my path. I did not believe that meeting a realtor in recovery was a random event or a coincidence. The realtor and I both attended the same meeting together and afterwards, she showed me a studio in the Central Business District in the downtown area, the Cotton Mill Condos on Poeyfarre Street in the city block between Constance and Annunciation. The red brick exterior and the rows of rectangular square-glass windows that lined the building revealed its warehouse origins. I liked the feel of the place and moved in.

Realizing the importance of spending Christmas with my family, I travelled to Michigan to celebrate the holidays and do some snowmobiling. Once I got back to New Orleans, I started establishing a new foundation. I attended recovery groups and connected with OSU alumni. I looked at potential places to set up a store.

RSS was also solidifying a firm foundation, and it was growing. In mid-January, I set sail on RSS's first national incentive cruise, with about 100 others, including leadership and dealers, to the Caribbean. In February, Valter visited me in New Orleans and we attended the Mardi Gras festivities and we did it sober. I also sailed on the Buckeye Cruise for Cancer which benefited the Urban and Shelley Meyer Fund for Cancer Research at OSC. Urban Meyer, who also attended the cruise, happened to be OSU's football coach at the time. When I got back to New Orleans, I learned that Aaron wanted to open a store again and that he was coming to New Orleans, so we swapped places. He took the condo and opened a store, and I went to South Carolina and stayed at Scott and Daphene's house for two weeks, helping Daphene's sister open a BoxDrop® Location.

Finally, on March 15, 2017, I got the wonderful news. The lawsuit with Mattress by Appointment had been settled. The case had been resolved and Mattress Direct had been dissolved. In a separate lawsuit, MBA was ordered to settle to pay RSS in order to continue operating, which, to me, was irony at its best. I was now free to return to Florida.

For the first time in a long time, I felt fantastic, light, and free.

"Darren, look. I know they sued you and wiped out your bank accounts and that you were put into this position. I will make sure that you get back to where you were and better." Those were the words that Scott had spoken to me long ago, and now they had come to light. I was back in Jacksonville Beach, living in a condo with an ocean view and was now employed as Chief Marketing Officer and Vice President of RSS.

In reflecting on the past 20 years, I realized I had been trying to direct the ship. I wanted to be the captain. But the captain must go down with the ship. I had done that. Many times. I had to let the business I created go and direct the Mattress

Direct dealers to a potential new ship, RSS, if they chose to embark upon it. Throughout this adventure, and I choose to see it as an adventure, I had forged a path for myself, even when I could not see what was in front of me. I had to learn how to be patient and how to be humble. I had to keep moving forward, sometimes blindly, with hope and with faith. When I surrendered the idea of being the captain, and instead became a part of the crew, my life took a dramatic turn for the better. The waters were no longer rough, and the course became narrow and straight. Scott was the captain now. I was no longer in charge. In fact, I had never been, at least not until I surrendered.

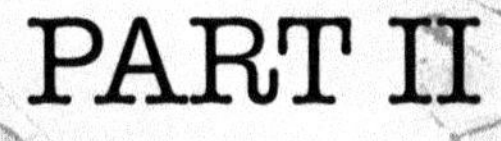

PART II

Sobriety

Chapter Ten

When I was six years old, my father asked me to go along with him on a car ride. It was an unusual request because Dad rarely asked me to tag along. In fact, I hardly ever saw him because he was hardly ever home. I hopped into the front seat, and we drove through the streets of Upper Arlington, an affluent suburb of Columbus, Ohio, where my parents had just bought a new home. Upper Arlington was the hometown of both of my parents. Dad had been a student at nearby West High School and Mom had attended Upper Arlington High School. It was where I had been born, so it was my hometown, too. Dad looked in my direction and said to me, "Darren. You're going to be the man of the family now."

Steve Conrad, my dad, had graduated from The Ohio State University's ROTC program beginning his career as an intelligence officer for the U.S. Army. A few months after I was born in March 1970, my dad was stationed in Berlin, Germany, and my mom, sister, and I moved overseas. From there, we moved to Fort Devens in Massachusetts, then to Fort Huachuca in Arizona.

I looked at Dad. His face looked sad. What did it mean that I would be "man of the family"? I was not exactly sure, but it did not take me long to figure out that Dad would be gone for a very long time. To console him, I put my hand on his leg and patted him. "Everything is going to be okay, Dad," I said. I was not sad. In fact, I felt a sense of relief. Shortly after that car ride, Dad was deployed to Korea for eight months.

After Dad left, I became more independent and self-sufficient. My sister, who was two years older than me, took on a mother's role and looked after me. We did not have the best of relationships, however. Mom worked several jobs and I rarely saw her. Sometimes at night I would sit by the phone waiting for her to call, wondering where she was and when she would be coming home. At that time in my life, I felt a lot of uncertainty. I feared being abandoned and I feared being alone.

During the day, my mom worked as a make-up artist for Christian Dior. In fact, she did the make up for one of the local news people in Columbus. She sold fine jewelry. And, she also had a small cleaning business. Eventually, she became employed with the Ramada Inn as an Events Coordinator for the hotel chain. Mom also sang at the local bars. She was very theatrical and had a beautiful voice. Both of my parents had been blessed in that department. Dad had been a theater major in college and had a nice singing voice as well.

When Dad returned from Korea, my parents divorced. They were only in their late twenties at the time. Dad then moved to northern Virginia where he worked for the NSA in the Pentagon for the next eight years. He never lived in our home in Upper Arlington. Mom set out to find her Mr. Goodbar, a man who would make everything okay again.

Holidays were an important part of our family life, and extended family gatherings were a big part of our celebrations. My mom took great care to make sure that every holiday was an amazing experience for my sister and me. The Easter bunny would visit and hide colorful eggs and chocolates throughout the house. We would spend hours looking for them, as well as the large Easter basket that we shared. On Christmas, my mom would put us to bed early because Santa Claus would be coming down the chimney at night. In the morning, we would open the special gifts he left for us under the tree. Decorating the tree was a big production and so was decorating the house. Looking back on it now, I feel that Mom really put her heart into making us feel valued as her children.

When I was twelve years old, Mom took my sister and me to the World's Fair in Knoxville, Tennessee, which was about 350 miles south of us. We drove in her VW Bug, which she bought for $500. It was not in the best of shape. We spray-painted it bright yellow in our driveway! The floorboard had holes in it and I could see the highway whiz by beneath our feet. Our plan was to meet my grandparents at a chalet in Gatlinburg, which was southeast of Knoxville. The terrain was mountainous and green, and looked more majestic than the rolling hills of southern Ohio.

That year, the World's Fair was called the International Energy Exposition and was held at the World's Fair Park in Knoxville. The theme was "Energy Turns the World." The first thing I noticed was a very tall structure, that looked like a truss tower with a golden orb, or hexagon, on top. It was called the Sun Sphere Tower and was 266 feet high. We saw all kinds of new inventions like touch screen displays and paying for gas at the pump. We tasted Cherry Coke and played video games like Pac Man and Space Invaders and Donkey Kong. On the trip back home to Ohio, as the sky darkened and my eyelids grew heavy, the humming of the wheels spinning on the road lulled me to sleep. I'm not sure how long I was asleep but my peaceful slumber did not last long after the car engine blew up! Mom pulled to the side of the road, and we waited in the car, watching the headlights of the oncoming traffic approach us and the taillights of those passing us by fade into the darkness. A tow truck driver finally arrived, and the Bug was secured in the back of his rig. The three of us rode up front in the cab with the driver, who dropped us off at a little country bar where we waited for our uncle to pick us up. Sis and I were hungry, but Mom did not have any money, so we ate crackers and drank water. Mom kept looking at her watch, drumming her fingertips on the tabletop. My sister was also getting anxious. I was not sure what to do, so I pulled a napkin out of the napkin holder and asked Mom if she had a pen. Thankfully, she did. I started drawing a hangman scaffold and the lines for a four-word phrase. "Let's play hangman," I said with a smile. My mom and sister started laughing and my sister asked if it there were any "a's" in it.

"Yes, there are," I said as I wrote __ ____ __ **a** _ **a** __.

Mom and sis kept guessing and I kept filling in the blanks or drawing a head, a body, and arms on my hangman. Then, Mom said she knew what the phrase was.

"VW does it again," she said. *Just like the commercial on T.V.*

We all started laughing. I wanted to keep things light and joke around. Life is always an adventure, so it is always best to remain upbeat.

Our uncle drove us back home to Ohio and we settled in. A couple of days later, my sister surprised my mom with something a mom rarely wants to hear. She was moving in with Dad. Her bags were packed and in two days' time she was gone. I had already grown accustomed to being on my own and adapting to new situations, but it was still a shock to me. At the time, I considered myself to be self-reliant but, in looking back, I know that God had been taking care of me all along. After my sister left, the house felt hollow. It was a bittersweet parting, but I knew it was for the best.

I was loyal to my mom and would never leave her. I always wanted to be there to support her. She continued dating, looking for her Mr. Right, but most of them turned out to be characters. Some of those guys just gave me a roll of quarters and said something like "Hey kid, go play some video games." Suffice it to say those relationships did not last very long. Mom was looking for a man who could be a potential life partner.

Divorced families were rare in Upper Arlington. I often felt out of place, but playing sports helped me to feel as if I fit in. Drinking alcohol did as well. Both sides of my family drank. To me, drinking alcohol was normal. I had no idea that there were adults who did not drink. If I would have ever heard of such a person, I would not have believed it. For me, adulthood was synonymous with drinking. I had already tasted alcohol at a young age. The 7th grade was when I started drinking heavily. My buddies and I would take a bottle of whiskey or rum from one of our parents' bars and mix it with juice. Or we would snatch some beers from the fridge. Drinking was an adult activity, and, at age 12, I was coming of age.

Mom met John Boutselis when I was 12 years old. John was 25 years old, nine years Mom's junior. I did not think anything of their age difference. To me, they were just adults. John was different than the other men that Mom had dated. He was a genuine person. He cared about me. He was considerate and mature. John took me camping. He let me hang out with him and his friends. He was very thoughtful, but he also was not afraid of disciplining me or letting me know if my mom did not approve of something. He always spoke on her behalf and he always had her back.

I looked up to John. I sincerely liked hanging around him and watching him follow his passion. He was, and still is, a gifted auto mechanic. His father had been a medical surgeon. John was a surgeon, too, only his patients were cars, motorcycles, and engines. He did not need a manual to know how to take a machine apart and put it back together again. He instinctively knew how to do it. I am not a car person or into mechanical things, but it was fun watching him do something he loved.

Another person I looked up to during my teen years was Keith Helfer, my best friend Joe's dad. Joe and I would catch our own bait and fish in the rivers. Keith had hundreds of fishing poles, and he made his own lures. To me, the Helfer family represented stability. They were the All-American family. Joe's parents had been married a long time. He had an older brother and an older sister. Keith Helfer had a successful printing company in Columbus. I was attracted to his success. He was always having fun and enjoying life. The best advice he ever gave me was that attitude is everything.

Mom, on the other hand, rarely talked about finances, but I knew she was worried about money. In the years following the divorce, the power would go off, and we would all sit in the dark until she could pay the electric bill. If I asked her to buy me something, she would say we could not afford it. From a young age, I promised myself that I would never live that way when I got older. I also knew that if I worked hard, I would make money. So, I raked leaves, shoveled snow, and had a paper route. When I was 14 years old, my mom mentioned that she liked a Patagonia ski jacket that cost somewhere in the neighborhood of $300. "It's just not something we can afford," she said. I worked hard and bought her that jacket for Christmas. The look of joy on her face when she opened my gift was worth it. I wanted her to know that in this life you *can* get what you want. I never wanted to set any limitations in my life, and I did not want her to have any in hers. That jacket was a symbol to show my mom that if you want something, you can get it. I wanted her to know how valuable she was to me.

Even though on the surface I seemed to be a happy-go-lucky kid, my life was becoming harder to manage. I could not focus and I was not doing well in school. On my 16th birthday, I decided to drop out of school and run away. A classmate and I had planned to drive to Florida, but when her dad found out about our plans, he put a stop to them. So, I went to the OSU campus looking for a party. I had my first intimate encounter with a girl. Wow! After that, there was no turning back.

After a week of partying, my money ran out. I came home. Mom picked up the phone and called the police. She told them I was an incorrigible runaway and asked them to pick me up. I spent the entire day at the police station talking to a social worker, then went to live with my grandparents. I dropped out of school. I also kept drinking and partying. Despite my behavior, my family loved me and was concerned about me. *"What are we going to do about Darren?"* was often the topic of conversation. Eventually, the decision was made that I would move to Arizona to live with my father at the beginning of the next school year.

After four years of dating, Mom and John had decided to marry. Before I left for Arizona, I attended their wedding on

August 8, 1986. It was the first time I ever wore a tuxedo and a boutonniere. My sister was in the wedding, too. My grandparents attended as well as John's parents, and my aunts, uncles and cousins. The women were dressed in white, lacy formal wear, and the men wore tuxes or suits. That photograph is the last one I have with all of us together. We all looked so happy. I looked like an innocent kid, rather than the wild child that I was.

That year in Arizona also had its challenges, including getting neurosurgery and getting kicked out of Dad's house. I returned to Ohio, but a lot had changed since I left. John had opened his own business, Boutselis Auto Care, on Livingston Avenue in east Columbus, and Mom was now helping him grow the business. My baby brother John had been born, and I became his babysitter, bottle feeding him and changing his diapers while my mom and John worked.

That summer, before my senior year, I started a lawn care business. I mowed and edged our lawn as well as my grandparents' and neighbors' lawns. Because everyone had their own lawn equipment, there was no overhead. Everything I made was pure profit. One afternoon, as I was cutting my grandparents' lawn, an older man driving a truck pulled to the side of the road. "Hey this is great," he yelled to me. "You should be doing this as a business." I stopped mowing and approached the man. He introduced himself as Bruce Anderson, owner of Lane & Kenny Body Shop. He said he would help me get business cards and my own lawn equipment. I thanked him and took him up on his offer. I had not done anything to merit his help. It was a random act of kindness.

When my senior year of high school started, I was 18 years old. All of my friends had already graduated and moved on, so I made new friends. Upper Arlington High School had a 96 percent graduation rate. Eighty-nine percent of its students continued on to college. So, I was motivated to get my high school diploma. Despite my desire to graduate, however, I missed a lot of school. Eventually, I had to attend a special study hall with three other kids. A school counselor led the study hall, which was similar to a recovery meeting, the goal of which was to help kids stop doing drugs and alcohol. That's how I met my friend Tommy. He was a junior, but he was two years younger than me. We got along so well that we went on a road trip to Sanibel Island and Fort Myers during Spring Break. There were also two girls in our study hall. One of them became my girlfriend for a time. Our counselor suggested that Tony and I attend a recovery meeting. That was the first recovery meeting I had ever attended. We saw a kid from school there, a popular athlete. I felt sorry for him. He was so popular and successful yet addicted to alcohol. This sadness did not extend to myself because I did not believe that I had a drinking problem. That study hall, however, was where the seeds of my future recovery were planted.

At age 19, I graduated high school. It was a major accomplishment for me, despite my brain injury from which I was able to recover and despite my incessant drinking and partying from which I was not. Mom and John bought a red brick century home on a 15-acre plot of land, complete with a barn and a pond in Groveport, and put the Upper Arlington house on the market. I moved into their summer house, a small one-room cottage with a wood-burning stove, paying them $20 a week so I could learn independence and responsibility before venturing out on my own.

Chapter Eleven

In the fall of 1989, I was flipping burgers and living the life of a young, precocious bachelor. Yes, it did not take Mom and John long to kick me out of the summer house. In hindsight, I am sure they had a good reason. The result of me being kicked out, however, was that I had nowhere to go. My solution to this newfound problem was to call Tommy, my friend from high school, and ask him if he wanted to rent an apartment in town together. Tommy was in his senior year of high school and the thought of having access to an apartment, intently as a place to party, was too good of a deal to pass up. Our apartment quickly transformed into one with revolving doors, with people coming in and people going out. In other words, Tommy's and my living arrangement was extremely short-lived, only two weeks, if that.

Let's just say that Tommy and I parted ways because of a girl. Now, I was not the type of guy to go clubbing, but Tommy suggested we go out on the town late one night. I tagged along with him and happened to meet a girl named Vivian, who was a bit older and more mature than me, and who also happened to have an identical twin sister named Violet. They looked so alike that it was difficult to distinguish between the two girls. I am not sure how Tommy's girlfriend found out about our night out, but she was not happy about it. Even though Tommy did not cheat on his girlfriend, she assumed that he had. She was angry, upset, jealous, and wanted to get even with him. Using her feminine wiles, she tried seducing me one day when Tommy was not around, then made sure to tell him *her* version of the story. This did not go over very well with Tommy. Tommy was well aware that I was in a casual short-term relationship with Vivian because she had already moved into our apartment. He never tried to pick a fight with me or anything like that. He just packed his stuff and moved out. The revolving doors continued to turn, with Vivian becoming upset and moving out, and her sister Violet moving in.

During that time of my life, no one could have ever persuasively argued that I did not have a casual moral attitude. I would also have to agree. I drank way too much alcohol much too often, and I sure spent a lot of my valuable time chasing pretty girls. I felt as if the alcohol and the girls were contributing to my self-worth and value, which was certainly not true, but it was what I believed to be true. With Tommy now gone, I now faced a new challenge: Paying the bills. I could only flip so many burgers, which would still not pay the rent, and I did not have any friends that I could room with. Most of them were going to college and living in dorms on campus, and here I was living in a crummy, little apartment. That all changed a few weeks later, however, when I ran into a buddy, who showed me a flyer he had picked up at his college. It was an advertisement for a well-paying sales job, a group interview, and it caught my attention.

The two of us decided to go to the group interview together, which lasted about an hour, with a bunch of other college-aged kids. Vector Marketing was hiring sales reps to sell Cutco Knives, basically kitchen cutlery and accessories and sporting knives. Manufactured in America, the knives were shiny and sharp, with all the appearances of being a superior product. Mike Bella, the District Manager for Vector, gave what I thought was a phenomenal and professional sales interview. Not only that, Mike was also an impressive-looking man. He looked as sharp as those knives, like the cover on *the* book of success. Mike was wearing a well-tailored suit with an eye-catching $100 bill tucked into a money clip on his jacket pocket. He had a cool office. He had secretaries. He had a sportscar. To a kid my age, it looked like Mike had it all!

After the group interview, my friend and I and several others were invited for individual interviews. During my one-on-one meeting with Mike, he was warm and cordial. He also made selling look fun and easy, and I was convinced that I could be a successful sales rep for Vector. I was invited to take the next step which was to attend a three-day training session. On that first day about a dozen people showed up. Our first assignment was to bring a list of personal connections, people who might be interested in watching a presentation. The next day, everyone brought their lists, averaging around 15 to 20 people, which was probably a normal amount that most people would come up with, a list of a few family members and friends. But I was so pumped up that I created a list with 600 names on it! After receiving our training on selling techniques and getting acquainted with using the cutlery on the second day, we were told that in order to give sales presentations to the people on our lists, we would either have to rent or purchase a knife kit for $200, which was quite a bit of money for a college kid back in 1989. The price of the kit did not stop me because I saw the value of owning it, considering it to be an investment rather than a liability. But I must say that a lot of the kids dropped out due to the cost, seeing that by the third day, our group had diminished to just a few sales reps.

Vector Marketing, still in existence today, is a single-level marketing company that promotes and sells Cutco knives. Cutco has been around since the 1940's, manufacturing quality knives in their Olean, New York factory. For the most part, Vector focuses on recruiting college kids on summer break who want to make money through the art of sales. Once the students complete the three-day training, they make appointments with potential customers and do demos in the customer's home. Even if a sales rep does not make a sale, they get paid for doing the demo. If they do make a sale, they receive a 15% commission.

With my training completed, I now had the opportunity to earn additional incentive prizes through a program called Fast Start. If I did 80 appointments, I would receive $15 per appointment. I called my mom and told her about my plans, but she was not as enthusiastic as I had hoped. "You can't make money selling knives," she said. My grandfather, on the other hand, supported me, telling me that I could make quite a bit of money if I excelled in sales. He believed in me, which contributed to my own belief that I could be successful. For additional motivation, I bought a copy of Zig Ziglar's book, *Secrets of Closing the Sale* by Zig Ziglar, read it in an entire night, then charged into my presentations like a lion for my first 40 appointments. The result was, surprisingly to me, 0 for 40!

But I did not go out as a lamb. Instead of giving up, I envisioned this experience as a learning opportunity. I talked with Mike about it, and he told me that I did not need to "sell" the knives because the knives would sell themselves. I knew that Cutco knives were a high-quality product which save customers time and money, and that that should be enough to convince customers that they needed them. In addition, Mike suggested that I read Dale Carnegie's *How to Win Friends and Influence People*, the message of which focuses on being genuine, authentic, and helpful. So, for the next 40 appointments, I changed my approach. I acted like my natural self and let the knives do the selling. Sure enough, people started buying.

My self-confidence not only hit the roof but went through it. It did not take me long to make $1,000 in sales resulting in a promotion as an Advanced Sales Rep. I kept making appointments, giving presentations, and people kept buying, buying, buying. When I achieved $2,500 in sales, I became an advisor and was mentioned in the national newsletter. That was a big deal to me. Vector was big on recognition. Recognition motivated me even more than money ever could because I craved validation. Mike Bella continued to mentor me, referring me to the teachings of Tony Robbins as well as Neuro-linguistic programming (NLP), which, in general, asserts that our thoughts and words are powerful enough to create our present and future reality. Mike was all about attitude, just like my friend Joe's dad had also said long ago, and I wanted to be just like Mike.

During my first year, I sold more than $40,000 in product, becoming one of the top sales reps in the company. I was promoted and started receiving 50% commission, becoming Mike Bella's right-hand man as the Assistant District Manager. I was earning around $1,000 per week, quite a bit of money for a 21-year-old kid during the early nineties. I photocopied one of my checks and wrote, "You can't make money selling knives" and mailed it to my mother. Needless to say, she called me to congratulate me, happily surprised that my new business venture turned out to be successful. She was proud of me and that continued to fuel my success. I continually worked hard at becoming more efficient. In order to make $1,000 per week, I had to make 10 to 12 sales, which would require 20 appointments. I did the absolute minimum to make money and I continued to advance. With the money I made, I bought nice suits and ties and splurged on a $300 Mont Blanc fountain pen. I bought a new car, a 300ZX with T-tops and leather interior, and a digital dashboard with a talkie that told me when my fuel level was low. I wore a money clip with a $100 bill on my front jacket pocket, just like Mike Bella did. By my second year, I had sold more than $100,000 in product. Direct sales was not a profession that people usually engaged in, but I was successful at it, which boosted my confidence even more.

Around that time, a guy named Jack joined Vector Marketing as a sales rep. He was from out of the area and did not know many people in Columbus. I took him under my wing and helped him find leads. All the while, I continued drinking and partying like a rock star. I felt as if I was living in a forever spring break kind of environment.

I was 22 years old when I was promoted to District Manager, the same level Mike Bella had been when I had first started with Vector Marketing. By this time, Mike had become Division Manager. It was now time for me to start my own office. But, where? I decided on Strongsville, Ohio, a southwest suburb of Cleveland, Ohio. Jack opened an office in Mansfield, Ohio, which is between Columbus and Cleveland. Another one of my friends started an office in Rocky River, a northwest suburb of Cleveland on the shores of Lake Erie. Once I got to Strongsville, I rented an office space, bought office furniture, and hired secretaries. As a District Manager,

I no longer worked directly for Vector Marketing. I was now considered an independent contractor. No longer in the business of selling knives for Cutco, I was now in the business of recruiting college kids to sell knives for Cutco.

I quickly learned how to conduct interviews and became successful at launching salespeople. I had realized and was living my passion: Recruiting and building teams, networking, and getting people together to achieve a goal! That summer I had 350 sales reps, becoming one of the top recruiters in the country and receiving a national recruiting award. My business also became one of the top ten branches in the company, which resulted in higher commission and higher pay. I had evolved into a completely different person than the young man who had once been flipping burgers and living the bachelor lifestyle in a little apartment.

The summer that I started my office in Strongsville, I also met a girl who would change my life for the better. Her name was Anna, a college student at Ohio University. The instant she walked into the office I was attracted. She had a different aura. She was sweet, beautiful, and different from the other girls I had known. She interviewed for a sales rep position, and within several weeks, we started dating. We got along well and spent a lot of time together.

With summer coming to an end, the college kids started going back to school. The office stayed open because I had some sales reps who did not attend college, but we were not as busy, and our sales were not as significant. Even though Anna returned to the university, we continued to date for the rest of the school year. I would make the four-hour drive, just to see her and attend her sorority events with her. During the holidays, we spent time with her family. They lived in Seven Hills, Ohio, and were of Polish descent. The Cleveland area was filled with pockets of ethnicity, especially on the west side. The delicious Eastern European foods that they made like pierogi and sauerkraut were wonderful.

The next summer Anna returned to Cleveland and became one of my key people. She was a good influence on me, and I felt lucky to have her in my life. She did not like to party, and I did not even try to sleep with her although we had been dating for more than one year. She was innocent. That summer the business was more successful than ever. But, like all summers, they pass too quickly. With the end of summer approaching, Anna, and all of the other college kids, would be going back to school, and I would be staying at the office, supervising the skeleton crew. I started to feel a longing to go to school, too. I was intelligent enough to attend college. I just was not disciplined as a student. And even though I was making good money, it was no longer motivating me to stay in the business. I wanted to earn a college degree and have the same college experience that everyone else was having. So, near the end of the summer, I talked to Anna about attending college, and she helped me fill out an application to The Ohio State University, my dad's alma mater.

That fall, Anna did not go back to Ohio University. Instead, she studied abroad in Europe. I missed her so much I could not stand to be away from her. I purchased an airline ticket and a Eurail pass and flew to France on a whim. She and I travelled by train visiting cities like Rome, Florence, and Venice in Italy, Prague in Czechoslovakia, and Salzburg in Austria. I bought her a gold ring, kind of like a promise or pre-engagement ring. We were in love! We walked hand-in hand down the cobblestone streets, surrounded by medieval architecture and domed churches, talking about the names of our future kids. When we were riding the trains, people would look at us and smile. They gave us bottles of wine or money to buy bottles of wine. In Venice, we had a very romantic dinner at a small restaurant with only three little tables. The lady who ran it lived upstairs. She did not speak English and neither of us spoke Italian, although Anna spoke French, so she was able to understand some Italian. The woman brought us a pitcher of wine and plate after tempting plate of delicious food, serving us a seven-course meal. In Rome, we ascended the helical staircase ascending and descending into Renaissance history, which was a challenge to me due to my fear of heights, but also a blessing.

It was easy to find an inexpensive hotel in Europe. We stayed at bed and breakfasts that served cold cuts and bread rolls and little soft-boiled eggs in cups in the morning. Everywhere we went the food was natural and healthy. The hotels there were different than in the States. In one of our rooms, there was a small shower that looked like a see-through tube. One morning when Anna went to get us some breakfast, the cleaning lady came in and just went about her business while I was showering. We were in Europe. Life was light. Life was carefree.

We ventured through winery after winery on the French side of the French-German border. In the city of Colmar, we rented a car. We were asked for our driver's licenses, but neither of us had one, so I just made a number up and they gave us the keys. From Colmar, we drove to Alsace and Strasbourg, collecting bottles of wine to take back home. That Christmas, everyone got a bottle of wine. In Europe all I ever drank was wine. I never thought about getting drunk. I never felt the itch nor the inspiration. Wine was the potion that connected Anna and I.

After those two magical weeks in Europe, I flew back to Cleveland. In my mailbox was an acceptance letter for OSU for Winter Quarter 1994! The admission was provisionary because I had not taken any college entry exams. Anna returned, we spent Christmas together, then I closed the business and moved back to Columbus where I rented a one-bedroom efficiency on 13th Avenue, considered by many to be a ghetto. It had one room, one futon, and one hundred cockroaches. It was always dark inside, and outside it was always gloomy and cold. It was the winter quarter at OSU after all. I did not know anyone at the school. And I did not have any experience in how to study. Attending classes was overwhelming. There were hundreds of students who attended classes in large lecture halls. I did not go to my final exams and received a 0.0 that quarter!

My parents, Anna, and her family were so excited that I was going to college that I could not bear to tell them about the 0.0. But, at OSU there was something called "freshman forgiveness," where you could retake the classes you took the first quarter. *There's hope, I thought. There's a chance.* I happened to start talking with Jack about this problem when he suggested that I join a fraternity. I was older than most of the kids, but I pledged to Sigma Phi Epsilon anyway so I could become a part of something bigger. To be an active member, I had to have a certain GPA, so it motivated me to study. I received a 3.2 the next quarter. Now I felt as if I was finally on my way to earning a B.S. in Human Ecology. I wanted to earn a college degree and that was the easiest path to receiving a diploma. I had never been guided in any way toward this major. I just wanted to earn my degree.

When I had first pledged to the fraternity, it had been in the process of restructuring. By the next quarter, I became the VP of recruitment. In looking back, it is interesting how life leads us, in any environment, on the same path. My passion was recruiting people, creating teams, and devising plans for success, whatever those plans looked like. I had been doing that for Vector Marketing. Now, here at Ohio State University, I was given another opportunity to build a team in my fraternity. I found myself again in the recruiting business.

Eventually I became good friends with the fraternity president and the controller. We built the fraternity to 150 members. Our fraternity house could hold only 56 guys, however. The other members lived in dorms on campus or at off-campus apartments. Our house had an academic advisor, a house mom, a graduate student, and an excellent cook. Because of our infrastructure, we won all-academic awards, sports awards, and had guys in the Student Affairs Office. We had everything we needed to be one of the power houses, and we certainly were. Out of 50 houses on campus, we were always in the top five. During those college years, I also met my best friend, Tony, and developed a small circle of friends including Sean and Nick. These were loyal friends, and we did everything together, from playing sports to drinking.

Now that I was no longer running a business in the summer, Anna opened the door for me to another team-building opportunity. She told me about a job at Hastings Middle School, one of the two feeder middle schools to my alma mater, Upper Arlington High School. It was a coaching job for the 7th grade girls' basketball and volleyball teams. Surprisingly, I was hired. There were 50 girls at the tryouts. I cut the team down to 10 for basketball and 12 for volleyball. Needless to say, the parents were not happy about that, but I wanted to play everyone equally. All three teams made it to the championships. We were 47-6 combined for the three-season record. My goal in coaching was to make the experience fun for the girls and help them enjoy the sport.

During my Vector years, I had accumulated a lot of impressive-looking trophies that were cluttering my apartment. I no longer had any use for them, but I did not want them to go to waste. At the end of the season, I would ask the girls to vote for Most Valuable or Most Improved Player, and other categories as well. I put those names on the trophies and awarded them to the girls at the sports banquet in addition to the gold medallions they received from the school. The parents were delighted. They called and told me what a big impact receiving the giant trophies had made on the girls.

In 1995, Anna graduated from college and came to Ohio State University to study for a short time. That is when she found out I had been involved in other relationships. At the time, it felt natural to me, and I never felt as if I would get caught. Anna was deeply hurt but willing to give our relationship another chance. For Christmas that year, she gave me an 18" x 11" chalkboard that read, "Clean Slate." Although her intentions were good, the truth was that I lived in a fraternity house and drank every night. It was one of the best ways to recruit guys to a college fraternity, at least during the 1990's. Wednesday through Saturday nights we had parties with the sororities, which looked like scenes from the movie *Animal House*. I was trying to be the big shot, hooking up with different girls from different sororities, being the guy that they thought was cool. It became apparent that Anna and I were now on different paths, and our timing was off. She had already graduated and was building her career while I was still in party mode and did not want to give up the college life that I had craved for so long. I wanted to be like everyone else and I did not want to be limited by a serious relationship. I certainly did not want my ability to drink to be limited, and I certainly did not think I had a drinking problem. Drinking was more important to me than preserving a relationship.

However, during my junior year, my fraternity brothers told me they thought I had a drinking problem. That is pretty significant when your frat brothers tell you something like that. On Big Brother night, which is when the pledge of the fraternity picks a big brother, the big brother takes the little brother out for a drink. That night I took my new little brother and the girl I was dating at the time, Stephanie, to a bar in my 300ZX. I had a suspended license, which I usually did have during that time of my life. We were driving back to the fraternity house late that night, my girlfriend and little brother in the passenger seat, when I saw police car lights flashing behind me. I knew that if I pulled over, I would get into trouble for driving with a suspended license. So, I turned off the headlights and floored it back to the fraternity house. This resulted in an incredible police car chase with seven or eight cars tailing me. As soon as we made it back to campus, we were surrounded by red and blue flashing lights. This ruckus at 3:45 a.m. woke up everyone in the fraternity house. My girlfriend and my little brother jumped out of the car, and I jumped into the passenger seat, but that plan did not work. I was arrested and hauled off to jail. Stephanie bailed me out the next morning, and I hired an attorney who got me off with reckless operation because I had never performed a breathalyzer test. Yes, after this night, my fraternity brothers told I had a drinking problem. But what was more of a problem was that I was not ready to surrender to alcohol just yet.

Chapter Twelve

"I don't know if I'm going to graduate, Dad." Dad was having his first drink of the day. I was on my fourth. Maybe my fifth.

It was October 2, 1998. A sunny autumn afternoon. The party was just getting started, and I was enjoying the warm weather with about 200 guests who had all gathered at Mom and John's farm. My dad, Steve, who was now living in Georgia, made a special trip to be there. My older sister travelled to Columbus as well. I was surrounded by my support system, a group of family and friends, as well as my fraternity brothers. I had asked Mom and John if I could have my graduation party at their place while the weather was still nice, and they were on board with it.

There were two people missing from this party, however. Two people who had made my going to college a possibility. The first one was Anna. She was the one who had been there when I expressed that I wanted to go to college. She was the one who had helped me complete my application to The Ohio State University. During the years that followed, our relationship faced many challenges. To put it simply, she did not like to party, and I did. She spent her time studying and preparing for her future. As VP of Recruiting for my fraternity, however, I was also preparing for my future, although I did not realize it at the time. Our paths had crossed long ago but now they no longer intersected.

Anna had been attending graduate school at a university several hours away, but I had not seen her in more than a year. I had made the trip there the previous year to see her in person. I explained that no matter how much we wanted our relationship to work, it was not going to. It was difficult to look at her, her deep brown eyes welling with tears. I told her things about me that would make her never want to see me again, let alone ever make her want to try to bring the relationship back to life. That day, I severed the cord, broke the bond, burned the last bridge. My life was now a new, clean slate. And so was hers.

While Anna had helped me get into OSU, it was my friend Jack, who had helped me stay the course. After confiding in him that I had earned a 0.0 GPA my first quarter, he suggested that I join a fraternity. Although our relationship felt strained at times, I felt as if Jack was an older brother who was looking out for me. But I did not invite Jack to the party because I felt he would not fit in with that crowd. At times, he could be negative and rub people the wrong way.

"What do you mean, 'not graduate', Darren?" Dad asked. He did not look angry, just surprised.

"French 102," I said, matter-of-factly, taking another sip of beer.

I needed a 2.0 GPA in order to graduate. If I did not get a "B" in French 102, then graduation day would not happen. At least, for me.

Dad did not say a word. There was no reaction. I immediately felt uncomfortable. “I’m failing French 102,” I explained further in an effort to break the uneasy silence.

Most students take their two foreign language requirements in succession, such as French 101 their first quarter, then French 102, their second. But not me. I took French 101 my first quarter, spent four years in college, then enrolled in French 102 my last quarter. Foreign languages do not come easily to me. To make matters worse, I had forgotten everything I had learned in French 101.

“I guess I’ve been busy with the fraternity,” I added.

“I see,” Dad said, looking at my fraternity brothers who were laughing and partying. He had a serious look on his face.

I had told Dad the truth. I had not been focused on school. Even the French 102 graduate teaching assistant advised me to drop the class. I told her, “I can’t do that.”

“Why not?” she asked. “You’re failing. You are still within the add-drop period. You can always try again next quarter.”

Her name was Linda. She was a straight arrow, a bookworm. She probably did not drink or smoke. I, on the other hand, was a typical fraternity guy. She and I were certainly not on the same wavelength. But something I said must have convinced her to work with me. I stayed in the class, and she helped me for the remainder of the quarter, taking the time to help me learn the material and do well enough on the final exam. I had never had anybody care about me that much. It gave me hope that I could finish and get my degree. I passed the class and graduated with a cumulative 2.000 GPA; the bare minimum needed to get my college diploma.

Graduation day was December 12, 1998. I was one of 10,000 students dressed in cap and gown at the St. John's Arena. "Darren Conrad," I heard the announcer say. I rose from my chair and walked toward the stage. It was an exciting feeling to shake the dean's hand and receive my diploma. I could not wipe the smile from my face as I waved to the roaring crowd, knowing that both my dad, Steve, and my mom were sitting there together watching me.

Through the crowd, I managed to find both of my parents after the ceremony, I looked at my dad. He had tears in his eyes. I have never seen my dad cry. Not even on the day he left us so long ago. He gave me a firm hug and said, "Darren, I'm so proud of you." I needed to hear that. Mom was smiling her broadest smile ever. She embraced me and told me she was proud of me, too. It felt good to see my parents together again, something I had not seen since I was six years old. Even though they were no longer together, I needed that validation from both of my parents on one of the most important days of my life. In looking back, I also realized that I would not have made it through those college years without God's help. When I was recruiting sales reps for Vector Marketing, I watched the college kids go back to school and developed a yearning to go to college. My previous girlfriend Anna and her family had encouraged me to go to school. When I was struggling, Jack suggested I join a fraternity. The fraternity required that I get good grades so I had to learn how to study. And, at the 11th hour, God had sent me a graduate student who helped me pass my French 102 class. It was apparent that God had put the right people at the right time in my path.

Now that I had a college degree in hand, I began interviewing with medical supply companies and pharmaceutical companies. I was not enjoying the process, however. I was not ready to leave Columbus to be a salesman and I was becoming frustrated. At that point in time, I received a call from someone in my past. Don Freda, the previous CEO of Vector Marketing.

"Darren. How about you come work for me?" Don had retired from Vector at a young age. In his early fifties.

Did I want to be a regional coordinator for Collegeclub.com, he asked?

Collegeclub.com was a website geared to college kids, a place where kids could create profiles and see what was going on in their schools and with their classmates. This was the beginning of the dot.com revolution. Silicon Valley was just starting to flourish.

Don explained that Collegeclub.com had hired a group of amazing IT people, but they did not have the marketing people they needed. As President of Marketing, he started calling everyone on his rolodex from Vector who might be looking for a new opportunity. Don's role was to duplicate Vector's success at College Club in the marketing and recruiting arenas.

At College Club, I found myself working with many of the same people I had worked with at Vector. As a regional coordinator, my mission was to get as many college-aged kids to join and use the website. My territory was Ohio, Kentucky, Indiana, and Pennsylvania. I hired campus reps to target the largest schools, such as OSU, UK, U Cincinnati, etc. We held on-campus events and handed out swag to promote the website. At the time, Sony was sponsoring College Club and had just come out with the Mavica digital camera. Sony sent new cameras to each of the regional coordinators. Dell also sent us laptops. I focused on using the digital cameras to get the kids engaged. I would take photos at the college bars, on campus, and in the dorms. In order to see the photos, the students would have to sign up for a free College Club account. But I did not do this all by myself. I hired campus reps and trained them on how to approach the students and get them to pose for pictures while they were hanging out with their friends.

This was a fun job. I had just graduated from OSU. Now I was back in school, except that I did not have to take any classes and, on top of that, I was getting paid for hanging out with college kids. I did very well with College Club. I had a $3,000 per month expense account and made $90,000 my first year. I bought my first home, a three-bedroom furnished condo on Bethel Road, just north of Upper Arlington. I renovated the home to include a fourth bedroom in the basement as well as an extra shower.

College Club sent its market reps to San Diego every three months. Awaiting us at the airport were double decker busses equipped with kegs. We would dine at fancy buffets serving crab claws and shrimp. College Club's downtown office had all the makings of futuristic Silicon Valley office, with ping pong tables and video games. This was the beginning of the tech world, and I was right in the middle of it. The IPO was about to go public. We had all been given stock options, so we were ready to become young millionaires.

Unfortunately, this adventure only lasted about one year. The IPO fell through, they laid people off, and the company closed. Although I do not think they went in the right direction, College Club did establish the foundation for another popular and well-known social media website, initially intended for college students, that has evolved over the years.

Throughout this time, Jack and I had still remained friends. While I was working for College Club, he had started his own business called Power Marketing Direct (PMD), selling mattresses from out of a storage unit. When he found out I was looking for work, he asked me if I wanted to be a sales rep. I told him that there was no way I would sell mattresses from a storage unit, so I rented a small showroom. I found an 800 square foot unit on Kenny Road and set up a store. I never signed any kind of contract with PMD. I worked as an independent contractor or 1099 with PMD as my mattress supplier. I did not receive any training. I ran my store based upon my knowledge and experiences from both Vector Marketing and College Club. I developed my own system for selling mattresses with a phone script, a tracking system, and low-overhead, easily making a six-figure income while giving my customers value. In a short amount of time, I had a lot of success and made a lot of money. My store had become the top location.

Jack was trying to duplicate his business but, in my opinion, he was not skilled at community-building or attracting others. I knew quite a few people who might be interested in owning their own stores. I wanted to help because I thought it would be good for everybody involved. I contacted all of the people I knew from Vector and College Club, inviting them to fly to Columbus, stay at my condo, and see my store. They saw firsthand the type of lifestyle that I had. It was attractive. Unlimited income, a great product, lots of free time.

That first year I grew PMD to around 50 locations; by the second year, that number had doubled. I was just a buddy who had paired up with another buddy to make things happen. They not only happened. They skyrocketed. Jack rented an

8,000 square foot warehouse directly behind the Kenny Road location, so I moved my store there.

In addition to running my own store as an independent contractor, I became PMD's national trainer, also working as an independent contractor, or 1099, for PMD. Despite my success, I felt that Jack was critical of me. He would come into my store and say negative things, mostly about how I had the store arranged, which I did not find incentivizing.

During the first year I had opened up shop at the Kenny Road location, a lady named Melanie walked into my store. Usually, appointments with customers lasted five or ten minutes. My appointment with Melanie lasted 45 minutes. We really hit it off. I could feel the chemistry between the two of us. Her hair was perfectly feathered, her nails long and manicured, her teeth were perfect. The pink sweater she was wearing looked as if it were pure cashmere. She looked like she could have been a cover model. I definitely wanted to see her again. Jack tried to discourage me by saying she was out of my league. But that did not stop me. I asked her on a date. She said her mother was in town. My answer to that was, "I can take both of you out." I had so much confidence that I did not take rejection. I took the two ladies to a bar, and we had some drinks and bar food. I learned later on that Melanie really did not like to drink, and that she had two children, ages 5 and 9. I was so mesmerized by her, and I really liked her kids. We dated for six months. I quickly maneuvered to make her my wife and I adopted her kids. I was in my early thirties and now I had an instant family.

Our courthouse wedding was on a November day. We spent our honeymoon on PMD's incentive cruise with 50 other people. Melanie and I signed up to play the Newlywed Game on the ship. We had a lot of fun and we won the game. It seemed as if we were destined to be together and that we were destined for success. We continued buying properties, purchasing a second home and renting the four-bedroom condo. Then, we bought an additional house, an even bigger one, and now had two rental properties. Life was going well. I had a beautiful wife, two nice kids, and a great income. My family did not care for Melanie, however. Nor did she and Jack get along. Melanie was not crazy about Jack either. She saw how I was growing PMD and had expressed to me that "I didn't need Jack." Jack, on the other hand, did not care for relationships. He was a single guy and was more interested in running PMD with a party attitude, which was not exactly the best type of environment to work in when you are a married man.

The inner circle at PMD was Jack, Jerry Williams, and me. In November 2002, Jack booked a leadership getaway for us to Aruba. While spouses were invited on incentive trips, they were not welcomed on executive trips. When I broke the news to Melanie, she told me not to worry about it, that she would schedule a fun trip for her and the kids while I was away. I expected her to be disappointed, but she was not. I found her response to be a bit strange but shrugged it off. At least she would not be sitting at home alone while I was away on a work trip.

We did not actually discuss business in Aruba, however. Instead, we bonded with each other through alcohol. Needless to say, with Melanie not there, I did a lot of drinking in Aruba. One night Jack made a comment that I would be better off without Melanie. At first, I thought he was joking around. He was the guy that said she was out of my league, right? Lately, I had been having doubts about my marriage. I did not know exactly why, however. So, his comment triggered further doubts. Did Jack know something about Melanie that I did not? I had called Melanie when I had first arrived in Aruba, but she did not answer her phone. She never did tell me where she and the kids were going on vacation, either. Jack insinuated that she was with me only for the money. She was not in the relationship for love. By this point in the conversation, I was totally hung over, convinced she was no longer good for me. I decided right then and there to end our marriage as soon as I returned home. For the rest of the trip, I considered myself as a single man, and I acted in ways that were not fitting behavior for a married man. This was not something I was proud of because I was still technically married.

When I returned to Columbus, I intended on breaking up with Melanie right away. I called and told her I would not be coming home and that I would be staying with Jerry Williams for a couple of days. She said she had just returned from her trip and that she would use my time away to get some rest. Again, when I asked her where she had gone, her answer was vague. I decided to stop by the house to end the relationship with her once and for all. Her face was red, and her eyes were swollen. She had been crying. Oh my God. This woman really did love me! I saw how vulnerable she was that day. Her usual rough exterior had faded. All I ever wanted to know was that she loved me, and now I knew that she did. I decided to stay in the relationship, and keep my indiscretion to myself, though it was eating me up inside. Still, I did everything I could to forget about it.

That fall Melanie and I attended all of the Ohio State University football games together and we flew out to Tempe, Arizona, for the Buckeyes' national championship game in January 2003. Jack also went to the game. He latched onto

Melanie and me like a lost puppy dog, barking orders and treating me like I was his servant. That was the tipping point. This was a personal trip, not a business one. When we got back to Columbus, I decided to leave PMD, and I began the process of coming up with a new plan for the future. I approached him and told him I was leaving.

Melanie was not the only one who believed that I did not need Jack to succeed. Jim, PMD's controller, also believed so. Jim was a smart business accountant. I did not have administrative skills. They were not that important to me. When he told me that he was planning on leaving PMD, we decided to start a business together. I had previously gone to the furniture markets with Jack and Jerry, and I remembered seeing an ad for a mattress manufacturing company, Park Place, that we had never used before. It was located in Greenville, South Carolina. I knew that there were no PMD locations there. Most people do not move to Greenville unless they are working for one of the companies there. Jim formed the company Carolina Direct, LLC, and we each put $5,000 into the business. He was planning on moving to Raleigh, North Carolina, and I, in turn, would move to Greenville, South Carolina. We would build the company in the Carolinas.

We flew to Greenville, South Carolina to meet with the mattress supplier at Park Place. He gave us the "D" pricing, which required $200,000 in sales. We had done well beyond that, so that would not be a problem. I sold our properties, cashed everything in, and bought a home in Greenville. I believed that Melanie and I could start a new life together there. Another clean slate. Instead of me leaving Melanie, Melanie and I were leaving. When I approached Jack for my final paycheck, he said I would have to sign a non-compete agreement in order to receive it. Up until that point, I had always been an independent contractor, as both a salesman and a national trainer. I needed my paycheck. It was money I had earned, so I had no other choice but to sign on the dotted line. Before I did, I made sure I had witnesses to this fact. I knew that this non-compete agreement was illegal. You cannot force someone to sign a document in order to receive their pay. Jack's actions only confirmed to me that leaving PMD was the right thing to do. He had been running his company based upon fear tactics and intimidation, rather than trust and team building. Melanie had been right. Working with Jack was not good for me.

Chapter Thirteen

I had never been to South Carolina, but I had heard it was a great place to do business. Ohioans usually flock to vacation spots like Myrtle Beach on the Atlantic Ocean to escape the cold weather and go to the beach, but we would be moving to the northwestern tip of the state. Situated between Charlotte, North Carolina, to the northeast and Atlanta, Georgia, to the southwest, the city of Greenville was bordered by national forests and the Smoky Mountains. It was small and quaint and had a population of less than 57,000 in May 2003 when I moved there. It was the perfect place, I thought, to reset our lives. I sold all three of our properties in the Columbus area and cashed everything in, buying a beautiful 3,500-square foot Lazarus-Shouse home in Greenville with five bedrooms and four bathrooms. Melanie would join me with the kids once they finished the school year.

As I was settling into the new place, I found out that my new business partner, Jim, was building Carolina Direct, LLC while still working as a controller for PMD. I was surprised because he had told me he was leaving the company. I had left the same company for many reasons, but the main one was to create something I believed in. PMD was doing things that did not align with my beliefs. Melanie's words of encouragement made me believe I could start my own business. That would, however, now be impossible to accomplish with Jim still on the books with PMD. I immediately ended my business relationship with him. And he ended our friendship. I did not feel bad about it. I knew I had made the right decision.

A company's culture is tantamount to its success. I wanted the new company to be a fun place to work but wanted the focus to be family fun, not partying fun. Honesty and integrity would also be the foundation of the dealer-customer relationship. I would not attract potential customers with misleading advertising then upsell them once they walked through the showroom doors. Instead, my company would provide a basic mattress that customers would be happy to buy, and vendors would be proud to sell. And, instead of intimidating my dealers or scaring and scarring them with litigation, I wanted to lead by example and build a community. I did not consider myself to be a chief but instead a warrior leading the way. I also listened to my dealer's suggestions on running and operating their businesses. I wanted to make them feel proud of their efforts and that they would be rewarded for them.

With Melanie in Ohio for the next month, and me now without a business to run, I started drinking every night. One night I got so drunk that I barely made it back home. I passed out on the couch. My wife had been trying to reach me, but I did not hear the phone ringing. She left the kids with her mother and drove 500 miles south from Columbus to Greenville. I was in a deep slumber by the time she arrived and was abruptly awoken by a loud knocking on the door. I cracked my eyes open. It was dark. I had no idea what time it was. Was it early morning? The next evening? Who could possibly be coming over? Was it one of the neighbors? I stumbled to the foyer, rubbing the sleep from my eyes, and looked out the window. It was my concerned-looking wife. My hair disheveled and my clothes wrinkled, I opened the door thinking what a sore sight I must be. Not saying a word, Melanie walked through the door and flicked on the lights. I am sure she could tell from my appearance that I was hungover. She walked into the kitchen, started clanking things around and got the coffee maker going. She brought me a cup of black coffee and sat next to me on the couch and did not say a word. She just looked at me, which was my queue to say something. I told her about the night before. How I had gone out drinking, got totally inebriated at a bar, and made some bad decisions. Her eyes widened with astonishment. I was expecting her to cry or call me names or throw things, but she just sat on the couch looking at me as if saying, "Go on. Continue." I decided to come clean and confessed what had happened in Aruba, too. After some time, she finally spoke. But she did not say much. All she said is that she would be back in June as we had planned, and she walked out the door.

Unsure if I was forgiven or not, I continued to move forward. I started a new company, called it Carolina Bedding, and rented a storefront just 10 minutes from the house. When Melanie came back one month later, she helped me with the business, especially with the administrative tasks, such as keeping the books and providing customer service. While working at the store, I started writing a training manual. It included everything I had contained in my head since working for Vector Marketing—Keeping the overhead low, providing a great product to the customer for a great value, and working with dealers who would be genuine, authentic, and good because customers are drawn to those qualities.

I created a product presentation that offered a nine-mattress line-up and focused on being better than the competition especially when it came to price. The products were designed to hit every price point. Most mattresses sell between $999 and $1999. My price point was always below $999. My strategy was simple: Listen to the customer to find out the problem and then solve the problem. I was there to connect with people and to help. I did not sell mattresses. Instead, I did exactly the opposite.

The mattresses started selling themselves. Everyone I met wanted to be a part of Carolina Bedding, the first ones being my neighbor, Tom, and his wife, who were more than happy to take over the store that Melanie and I had been running so that we could concentrate on opening more locations. One afternoon, a customer named M.H. came in and bought a mattress and expressed that he wanted to open a location in Charlotte, North Carolina. Another family opened a location in Shelby, NC, and another in Ashville, NC. With these new additions, Carolina Bedding now had a foothold in the Carolinas. What was interesting was that I had not put any effort into building the business, nor had I called upon my vast network of friends and acquaintances from Vector, College Club, or even OSU, like I had done to build PMD. I started from scratch. To me, it was evidence of the law of attraction at work.

Our bedding manufacturer, Park Place, was superior. It was a fourth-generation family-owned company. Our sales rep was cordial and easy to work with. Our company's growth was limited, however, to where Park Place could deliver, so that is where I focused on building the company. In a short amount of time, we had grown to 30 locations, stretching from the Carolinas and Georgia to Tennessee and Florida.

In early 2004, things started to get a little strange. I was checking my email one morning, when I received an email message from the address, carolinabeddingdone@yahoo.com. Curious, I clicked on it. It contained a strange poem, which sounded almost threatening in nature. As I continued to scroll through the message, there was a photograph of me with two girls in Aruba. *I suspected that there was only one person who could have sent that email.* I was relieved that I had come clean with Melanie and that we were moving past my previous indiscretions. A few weeks later, to my surprise, there was a knock at the door. I was being served with a lawsuit from PMD due to breach of dealer contract! I was not sure how Jack knew about Carolina Bedding but figured that it might have been from a mutual vendor.

Then, things really started turning sour. Melanie had not been getting along with Tom and his wife, our neighbors, the couple who had been running our first location. My drinking problem also did not help my relationship with the neighbors either. At a Halloween outing with them, I had gotten so drunk that my wife locked me out of the house. I still did not recognize at this time how my drinking was deeply affecting every aspect of my life. Our neighbors seemed like good and loyal people, but then it seemed as if Tom had turned from the light to the dark side in the form of a threatening voicemail message admitting that he had sent Jack a list of Carolina Bedding's dealer names and phone numbers. *That sure came out of left field!* He did end the message with a nice, friendly, "You're f***ed" however.

I did not respond to his voicemail message. Instead, I hired a high-power attorney and bought a new car, a Black Nissan 350Z, and parked it in the driveway right where I was sure Tom would see it. It was my way of telling him that not he nor anyone, especially Jack, was going to bring me down. After talking things over with my wife, Melanie and I decided to sell our Greenville home, which we both loved, to move to Jacksonville to be near my dad. It would be good to have some family support. Greenville had been a culture shock to us anyway. It was the deep south, so different from Ohio, and the kids had never been really happy there. I could also easily run the business from Florida.

In Jacksonville, we rented a house in a gated community called Eagle Harbor. My dad lived on the 17th fairway and we rented a house on the 18th. I also rented a 3,000-square foot warehouse on Western Way for the business. It had an office where Melanie could work and a store location from where I could set up a store. I started advertising, interviewing and recruiting people. That was part of the process I had created and grown since my days at Vector Marketing, throughout my years as VP of Recruiting for my fraternity, my work at College Club as well as my recruiting efforts for PMD. I had learned throughout the years how to attract people. It became more challenging to grow Carolina Bedding, however, because I was now in a legal battle. Despite this challenge, I never quit. My intentions were always to do good for the people who worked with me.

I had to travel to Ohio to attend a preliminary hearing for the PMD lawsuit because I had been ordered by the court to not do business within 100 miles of any PMD location. I got a map and drew circles around all of the PMD locations. Jacksonville was outside of that realm. So were the Carolinas and Florida. Jack, on the other hand, interpreted the injunction as meaning I could not do business within 100 miles of any *planned* PMD location. It seemed as if every time I opened a new location, he filed another motion against me.

This legal battle might have sounded like a brutal thing for me to endure but I still felt happy and content. I was living on a golf course, playing golf every day, making appointments on my score card all the while paying legal expenses. In the Fall of 2004, Carolina Bedding held its first incentive trip. Three couples attended in addition to Melanie and me: M.H., Shannon Turner, Tim Archer, and their wives. By February 2005, Carolina Bedding had grown to 40 locations.

Around that time, I decided to start another company similar to College Club, which I called Tailgate Photo. It was a dot com company tailored to sports fans. The Superbowl was being played in Jacksonville that year, and I figured it would be the perfect place to test my business model. I went to the game and took 400 photos of tailgaters and really had a great time doing so. People actually bought photos at the party! That night, I held a meeting with my web designer at the Eagle Harbor clubhouse to make sure the website would not experience any glitches with all of those orders coming in.

When I returned home, the house was empty and there was a note on the fridge. Melanie and the kids were leaving for good. *I was blind-sided.* Yes, Melanie and I had our disagreements on how to discipline the kids, but I thought we were doing okay. Not knowing what to do, I called my dad and told him that Melanie and the kids left me. He was heading to Las Vegas the next day for a conference and was taking his new wife with him and asked if I wanted to come along. Having visited Las Vegas many times, I had accrued travel points, so I set my dad and his wife up with a nice suite. I called Melanie and left her a voicemail message that I was going to Las Vegas with my dad and that I would not be home. I was expecting her to come back to the house, so I hired a private investigator. I wanted to see what she was up to. On the plane ride to Las Vegas, I was sitting next to a couple of women, telling them how Melanie had walked out on me. They suggested that she left me for another man. As soon as I got back to Jacksonville, I soon found out that the women's assumptions had been correct. The private investigator said that Melanie had been fully engaged in a relationship with a man while still living with me. She even had a relationship with his family. I immediately changed the bank accounts but I was too late. There was a charge for a trip to St. Thomas in the amount of $15,000. I had not gone to St. Thomas!

Living alone in that big house was emotionally painful, especially at night when it was dark. I could not stay there any longer. I rented a small condo nearby and drank myself to oblivion every night. I was also obsessed with finding out what my wife was doing. When I found out that she was living about 20 minutes away, I drove to the house and knocked on the door. She was just getting out of the shower when the kids let me in. When she saw me, she wrapped herself in a towel like I was a total stranger. "You're my wife," I said. She told me to go so I left. Still, I would call her on the phone repeatedly, wanting answers, but she would never take my calls. That was the worst part, her not telling me why. I felt as if I had been destroyed. I did not want to have multiple marriages. I wanted to have one marriage and stay in it, whether it was good or bad. But it was not up to me at this point.

I needed help so I started seeing a therapist. She suggested that I start going to recovery meetings. I followed her advice and, for the next 30 days I attended 30 meetings. It was difficult for me to identify with the people in the group, however. I empathized with them, but I did not believe in my heart that I was an alcoholic. Alcohol was synonymous with fun and everything in my life revolved around it: family, friends, fraternity brothers, work, OSU football games. Everything. With my personal life out of my control, I chose to focus on something within my reach, the building of Carolina Bedding. I immediately removed Melanie from everything and anything that had to do with the company and hired an administrator to work out of my home. Days turned into nights which turned into days and back into nights again as if I was on autopilot. Sometimes I would just lie with my eyes open in the dark at night unable to sleep. One particular night, there was no fan or air conditioner running. I was just lying there in silence looking into the dead of night. Suddenly, I felt a cool wind blow over my face. From where did it come? I did not know. For some reason, however, it made me realize that I was going to be okay.

Yes, I was still being sued, and, yes, my wife had left me for a young, fit personal trainer, and the kids were with her. My brain was on hyperdrive, but I kept telling myself, convincing myself, that I was going to be okay. I stayed in that small condo in Jacksonville for the next six months, continuing to grow the business, until our divorce was finalized in 2005. I was ordered to pay Melanie $6,500 per month in child support, even though I did not see the children. Melanie did not want me to see them, nor did they ask to see me.

With nothing left for me in Jacksonville, I drove 500 miles north to Greensboro, North Carolina, in a small truck packed with my belongings. My secretary followed me in my car, and I bought her an airline ticket to fly back to Florida. The city of Greensboro is in the middle of the state near the North Carolina-Virginia border, in what is called the Piedmont Triad; the cities of Winston-Salem, Greensboro, and High Point, all geographically close in proximity, create this triangle. I rented a small two-bedroom apartment on Big Tree Way, adjacent to a wooded area lining South Buffalo Creek. I rented a store location in Kernersville, about ten minutes away, with the intention of duplicating stores using my recruiting methods. When I was not working, I hung out by the apartment complex pool and made some friends there. My existence in Greensboro for the next six months was comprised of selling mattresses by day and socializing and drinking by night.

On the surface, it appeared that I left Florida to grow Carolina Bedding, but it felt more to me like I was running away. And, although my business was a one-man show, it continued to grow. I kept track of orders on a dry erase board that was in my living room and erased them when the dealers paid. It was a simple system and it worked for me at the time. Of course, there were some checks that bounced along the way. I had to spend time chasing dealers, asking them to make good on their checks. E.S., the Park Place sales rep, suggested that the dealers pay Park Place directly, then, in turn, Park Place would pay me. I let the idea simmer, but I did not act upon it because I liked being in control of the process. I continued advertising and recruiting potential dealers, interviewing them in local restaurants. The business was recovering, but, in my personal life, I remained in a dark place. No one knew that I was drinking every night to the point of blacking out. But drinking numbed me and it was the only way I could cope with Melanie leaving me.

One evening, out of the blue, Melanie surprised me with a knock on the door. She said she did not have any feelings for her personal trainer and that he never meant anything to her. We spent the night together and she gave me hope that we could reconnect and get back together. I was willing to do anything so she would come home. That would be better than wallowing in my lonely existence. I was struggling with the idea that I was divorced. I did not want to be divorced. But we did not get back together. On the business side of things, I could no longer afford attorneys and I did not want to fight in court anymore. I would keep building Carolina Bedding and if I had to file bankruptcy, then I would. Carolina Bedding had been doing between four and five million dollars in annual sales, and I was also being paid yearly bonuses by the manufacturer. So, I continued moving forward and growing the business.

After staying in Greensboro for six months, I moved to South Carolina. I rented a small, two-bedroom unit at Hidden Tree Apartments in Mount Pleasant, a little town near historic Charleston. My intention was not to open any stores there. I already had duplicated enough stores in the area. I just loved historical towns and wanted to experience living in Charleston. There was nothing for me in Florida anymore, so why not? I went on historic tours, haunted tours, and did a lot of sight-seeing.

Across the street from my apartment complex was the Strike Zone, a bar and bowling alley, where OSU alumni often met to watch the games. Every Saturday, I watched the Buckeyes play and connected with everyone. Eventually, I amassed a good crew of friends, enough to last for the entire football season. But, when the games weren't being played, I often spent time alone.

One evening, as I was trying to relax in my tiny, dark apartment, I got a phone call. On the other end of the line was the 25-year-old personal trainer that my wife had left me for. He said his name was Carl.

"Darren. I know you don't know me, but I have some news about Melanie."

"I'm listening," I said.

"I want to find out the truth," he said.

Carl and I started talking. He fired off questions and I provided quick answers. We immediately had built a rapport based upon a woman who had broken both of our hearts.

"I think we need to meet face to face," Carl said. It took me only a short amount of time to agree. Tomorrow, I said. Tomorrow, I would hop in my car and hightail it down to Jacksonville.

Chapter Fourteen

The next morning my mind was still reeling from the phone conversation the night before. It was daybreak when I dragged myself out of bed. The sun's rays filtered through my window blinds, waking me up. I took a cold shower, threw on some clothes, and hopped into my black 350Z without eating or drinking a thing. At least the drive from Charleston to Jacksonville would be a breeze—a straight-shot, four-hour ride south on I-95, but that would be the only thing I would do this morning that would be easy.

I felt confused as to why the man my wife left me for wanted to see me in person right away. What did he have to tell me that was so urgent? I walked down the steps to the parking lot, unlocked my car, and sat in the driver's seat. Before I put the key in the ignition, my foot on the gas, and revved the engine, I sat still. My heart was racing; my mind was cluttered with random thoughts. Who was this guy? Did he have an ulterior motive? Was he going to try and jump me? I could not convince myself that driving to Jacksonville to meet my ex-wife's boyfriend was a good idea, but my curiosity was overruling my common sense. Carl was 25 years old, about ten years younger than me. He was most likely in great physical condition because he was a personal trainer. I was the total opposite. I was out of shape. I was smoking cigarettes. I was drinking every day. Before we ended our phone conversation the night before, I suggested we meet in a public place, and he agreed. A popular pancake place came to mind, which was directly off of the interstate.

I headed west on Route 17, passing north of John's Island, Edisto Island, St. Helena's Island, and Hilton Head Island. Islands and rivers make up the landscape of South Carolina's eastern coast, contributing to its unique and beautiful geography. Crossing into Georgia, I passed through the outskirts of Savannah, one of the state's key historical cities that I had wanted to visit during one of my I-95 excursions but had not done so yet. I drove through the cities of Brunswick and Kingsland, Georgia, then crossed into Florida. There was no turning back. My meeting with Carl was now imminent.

Just before reaching the outskirts of Jacksonville, I pulled off an exit and made a right-hand turn. Yep, it was the right exit. Through the treetops, I could see the colorful, towering sign of the restaurant on a monopole, a beacon announcing the place where I would be meeting my nemesis face to face. My stomach muscles clenched. I was nervous and anxious. It was not an everyday occurrence for a man to be meeting with his wife's boyfriend, or should I say, ex-wife's, boyfriend. That she had left me for a younger, more fit man had chiseled away my self-esteem and inflicted what felt like irreparable harm to my ego.

I pulled into the parking lot relieved it was full of cars. I circled around the lot until I found a shady parking space under a Live Oak tree. Placing the vehicle in park, I kept the engine running and took a few minutes to breathe. I wanted to look and feel confident when I met Carl. Once I felt ready, if one can ever be ready for such an occasion, I got out of the car and walked toward the restaurant, passing a happy-looking couple walking arm in arm as if they were so in love that everything else in the world had disappeared. My legs felt as heavy as lead, but I kept moving forward. I opened the door and was greeted by a young hostess with a cheery face. Did I need a table for one, or did I want to sit at the breakfast bar? A young man sitting at a booth near the entrance with black, wavy hair looked in my direction. "I'm meeting someone here," I told her.

As soon as Carl saw me, he stood up, approached me, and shook my hand. He was more than six feet tall. Wide shoulders. Buff arms. "Darren, have a seat," he said motioning to the table in front of him. He looked like a genuinely nice guy. After what had happened with Melanie, I cannot say, however, that my trust barometer was working properly. He smiled, although somewhat tentatively. I scanned the restaurant. There was a cop sitting at the breakfast bar drinking a cup of coffee. The restaurant was crowded, nearly filled to capacity. The waitress, hair disheveled, looked overworked, like everyone had called in sick that day, except for her.

"Coffee?" she asked as she literally ran to the table.

"Yes, cream and sugar," I said. I usually drank two large cups every morning to combat hangovers, and I had been running on empty today.

"Sugar and cream are on the table, dear." She whisked by with several plates stacked on her arm. "I'll be right back with your coffee."

"Darren. Thanks for coming," said Carl. My attention shifted back to the reason I had driven four hours to get here. "I wasn't sure you'd want to meet with me, as you know . . . uh . . . but I'm glad you made the drive. I think there's something you should know."

"Go ahead, Carl."

"Well, I think Melanie has been doing to me what she has been doing to you."

"What has she been doing to *you*?"

"I think she has been using both of us!" The young man sitting across the table looked pained and heartbroken. It was obvious he had feelings for Melanie.

The waitress brought my coffee, accidentally spilling some on the table. "Sorry about that. Did you want to order anything?" she asked.

"No, just coffee. Thanks." I smiled and grabbed a napkin to clean up the mess. She sighed a breath of relief.

I took a sip of the coffee. It was cold and weak, but I drank it anyway, remembering the cup of bitter brew that Melanie had made me after she drove all the way from Ohio to South Carolina to check on me. That time she found me hungover and crashed on the couch still smelling of alcohol.

Carl indicated that he would like to continue the conversation, so I gave him my full attention. He explained how he had been Melanie's personal trainer at the gym. The last thing I wanted to hear were the details about their relationship—it stung—I only wanted to know what he had to tell me that could not wait. After working with Melanie for a few weeks, Carl continued, Melanie had started confiding in him, saying I was a bad husband and a no-good drunk, and that I had not been taking care of her financially. Those words felt like a dagger tearing my heart in two. Inside I was wincing in pain, but I maintained a blank expression. Carl continued his story that was beginning to sound more like a tragic epic poem. It was obvious he felt sorry for Melanie and had come down with a case of knight in shining armor syndrome. With each sad story she told him, he became more emotionally attached to her. I thought back to the day she had showed up at my apartment in Greensboro and spent the night with me, saying she had no feelings for Carl. Oh, how this woman played my heartstrings as well as his!

Carl finally got to the part that I had driven all the way from South Carolina to hear in person. He said Melanie had asked him to cash checks for her. At first, he said he did not think anything of it. The checks were not for large sums of money, at least, not in the beginning. But, as she continued to ask him to cash more checks, he said it did not feel right. Over a period of time, she had written checks totaling more than $50,000, keeping the money in a safe. I had trusted Melanie with the business and never had any suspicions of her whatsoever. I felt completely played and sick to my stomach.

To be fair, I had betrayed Melanie in our marriage as well. I imagined that my infidelity hurt her deeply, though she had never professed it had. Maybe, at the time, she was looking for a way to financially protect herself and her kids. But committing a crime was not the right way to do that.

Carl paused to take a bite of the cheeseburger he had ordered long before I had arrived on the scene. As he was eating, I thought about the tale this young man had spun, a tale of how I had been swindled and betrayed by someone I once loved. Everything I had thought was safe and true was actually the opposite. Our meeting ended shortly after that, with us exchanging phone numbers and email addresses and me driving back to Charleston. I was unsure of what my next step should be, so I contacted my divorce attorney upon my return.

Even though I had received the bad news, it still had felt good and natural to be back in Florida. There was no reason why I should not come back to live there, even though the lawsuit with PMD had lingered past the original injunction, with Jack continuing to file motions against me every time a new Carolina Bedding location opened. My dad was still living in Eagle Harbor and talked me into buying a home there. He suggested that I buy a house and put it in his name due to the lawsuit. I made the down payment and moved in. But it felt strange living there. The memories still lingered. Of Melanie and the kids. How we seemed to be happy there. And then, on that terrible day when I came home, and the house was empty. My wife and kids gone. My marriage over. Although my new home was beautiful, it just did not feel right living there.

A couple of weeks after I moved in, I happened to look out the front window and saw a strange sight. Melanie's car was parked in front of my neighbor's house. I opened the door and heard two ladies talking outside. I would recognize her voice anywhere. Melanie was outside chatting with the neighbor. I went back into the house, picked up my cell phone, and immediately called Carl. "Guess who is over my house?" Carl had ended his relationship with Melanie by now, and we had actually become friends, strange though it seemed.

"Who?"

"You busy? Come over and see."

In less than ten minutes, Carl pulled into my driveway. When I opened the door, he had a strange look on his face. "Let's toss a football on the front lawn," I told him with a smile. He got my drift. We went outdoors and started throwing the ball around, definitely wanting to be seen as friends and allies who had joined forces against her. The look on her face was priceless. It was worth it, though I admit it was strange hanging around Carl. I was still mourning the loss of my wife and he was feeling bad about the breakup with his girlfriend, who happened to be the same woman. That we had befriended each other somehow helped the pain go away.

My friendship with Carl was beneficial in another way as well. Through him, I learned that there are people who can easily live a sober life. He introduced me to his friends. None of them were drinkers. I would spend my weekends playing softball and having cookouts with people who knew how to have fun without drinking. I even went to a bachelor party and we never drank a drop.

Carl also helped me get the evidence I needed to support my case against my ex-wife, which was overwhelming. He had made copies of all of the checks and would be my star witness should I take Melanie to federal court. My divorce attorney was confident that he could negotiate a settlement and we did. The judge waived my parental rights (as I had adopted her children) so I would no longer have to pay Melanie $6,500 monthly in child support. After that, I considered my relationship with Melanie to be over. Forever.

Even though I was hanging out with Carl and his sober friends, I still acted upon my rebellious side. I started casually dating a girl named Tiffany whom I would say embodied the practice, if it could be considered a practice, of drinking. She was a hardcore Rockstar drinker, and, in fact, I think the only woman I have ever met that could outdrink me. This girl raised the bar in terms of wild and crazy. She would buy a case of beer, or Red Bulls, and Jägermeister and we would get really drunk. We flew to Hawaii for ten days and were drunk the entire time. Needless to say, the relationship was not suitable for the long term.

I knew that it was an out-of-control, hedonistic relationship, but I was so intensely attracted to her. She was beautiful and fun, and I became addicted to the craziness and adventure that our relationship encapsulated. But, at the same time, I also knew I had to get out. The only way would be for me to move. That is how I dealt with my alcoholism. I would just change my address. It had become the norm for me to move every year, sometimes every six months. My mom often joked that she needed a rolodex to keep track of my addresses. I knew that I was unstable, but I had a talent for building companies and earning income. So, I still did not see my drinking as a problem.

On Christmas Day 2006, I had a new start. I sold the house in Eagle Harbor, much to Dad's dismay, and moved into a 1,200-square-foot townhome on the beach. It was a duplex, but I only bought one unit. I had my own pool and a large fenced-in yard. It felt like it was my "spot", a place where I could create my own beach world. I built a new social network. I joined a volleyball league, got to know my neighbors, and connected with fellow OSU alumni in the area. I also bought a boat and hired a personal trainer. The move also helped me distance myself from Tiffany. But, although my relationship with her became distant, I still could not completely break away. I could not erase her number from my phone.

My new beach lifestyle, however, did not free me from drinking. It actually gave me the opportunity to take my drinking to a new level. On the Fourth of July, our neighborhood had a street party. My house was the third stop. My fraternity buddies came down from Ohio for the party. We spent the entire day drinking and playing yard games on the lawn at my house, just me and the guys, along with about 150 other guests. We also spent the night drinking at the local bars with my personal trainer and her friends. I felt as if I was back in college.

Once my college buddies went home, I continued drinking on my own. I believed that I had my drinking under control. I would abstain from drinking during the day. And, in the evening, I would let fate decide. I would play solitaire on my computer. If I won—and I usually did—I would go out drinking around 10 p.m. I had developed a routine of visiting the local bars. I swirled around Jacksonville Beach like I was riding on a carousel. At the end of the night, I would always end up at the same bar where I could buy a bottle of alcohol when they closed their doors at 2 a.m. The next morning it would always be the same. I would wake up hung over wondering where my car was. If I had not taken my car, I would search my apartment for my wallet then check my bank account to see what I spent my money on the night before.

The civil trial with PMD had ended. I just decided not to show up. Not because I did not care or that I thought I was guilty of the charges, but rather because I had been hemorrhaging money to the attorneys and could not get ahead. I had grown tired of fighting and did not think that either side would win. As a result of skipping the trial, I lost by default. A hearing was to be held in Columbus, Ohio, to decide the damages, so I decided to fly there to represent myself. At least, I might be able to have some sort of say in the outcome.

I used my "bar" time to study my case intently, writing questions on bar napkins that I would ask the witnesses, and questions that I would object to. I became so involved in my preparations that it got to the point where they consumed me.

Two of my good friends, who were also business associates, offered to drive to the hearing to support me: Joel drove from Madison, Wisconsin, and Cliff from Indianapolis, Indiana. We had all worked at Vector Marketing and PMD together. They left PMD shortly after I did and started a marketing company together. We had stayed in touch over the years, collaborating by sharing our annual incentive trip and our national calls. We had been working in conjunction with each other so our individual companies could grow.

I arrived in Columbus for the hearing, dressed in my best suit. I was expecting a jury, but, to my surprise, the judge said there would be none. I am not an attorney, so I was not aware of how the court hearing would be handled. I had only assumed. So, I presented my case to the judge for him to decide. I called my witnesses to the stand and cross-examined Jack. I objected four times and won three on my own. The hearing only lasted a few hours. At the end, I recall the judge saying he did not see any damages. He wished me safe travels back to Florida.

As I flew back to Jacksonville Beach, I chose to only see the positives. Because of the lawsuit, I had the unique experience of being an "attorney" for a day. No price could be put on that. Carolina Bedding was also doing well, business was booming, and we had grown to nearly 50 locations. I was doing several million dollars of business with our manufacturer, who was well aware of the lawsuit with PMD, but it did not affect our business relationship. I thought back to a casual conversation I had had with one of the reps awhile back. "You know, Darren," he said. "No one wins a lawsuit except for the attorneys. When you put yourself in the arena, you're putting yourself out there. You're going to be attacked when you have success." I flipped my seat back and closed my eyes, listening to the engines of the plane roar, feeling confident that things were going to go in my favor. It just felt good to be flying back home to Florida.

Chapter Fifteen

It was the "Third Saturday in September," and I was on a flight to Knoxville, Tennessee, seated next to a very pretty woman that I barely knew. The "Third Saturday" is a rivalry between the University of Florida Gators and the University of Tennessee Volunteers. This year the two Southern Conference teams would be playing at Knoxville's Neyland Stadium, a facility so large it can hold more than 100,000 fans. One of my Carolina Bedding dealers, Ramon, and his wife, who lived and ran a store in Knoxville, knew that I was a Buckeyes fan and invited me to the game. Since Ramon was attending the game with his wife, I felt as if I needed a date. I had not been dating anyone at the time so one of my dealers decided to set me up on a blind date with the woman who was now seated next to me. She was not the type of woman I would typically date. I am generally a happy-go-lucky guy and she seemed a bit pessimistic. Needless to say, there was not much of a connection between us.

The flight to Knoxville took about three and one-half hours and included a layover. When we landed at McGhee Tyson airport, we grabbed our luggage and waited outside for Ramon and his wife to pick us up. It was a smaller airport than Jacksonville's, so I believed that the couple would not have trouble finding us. Within a few minutes, a black Cadillac Escalade pulled up and the window on the passenger's side slid down. A nice-looking middle-aged lady smiled and asked if I was Darren. I said, "Well, yes." Upon my announcement, Ramon got out of the car and helped us with our luggage, and we climbed into the backseat. The couple asked us if we were thirsty and pointed to a pitcher of margaritas in the back. I looked at my watch. It was only noon. I normally refrained from drinking until the evening, but today was a game day so I would make an exception. Obviously, Ramon and his wife enjoyed a good cocktail. The Escalade took off and we headed to the tailgate party.

At the tailgate, we ate grilled steaks and drank more cocktails before heading to the OSU club. I cannot speak for my date, but I was pretty lit up due to drinking before we even got to the game. As we entered the gate, I looked at our tickets. The seats were high up in the stadium. As we climbed the steps, I could feel the effects of the alcohol setting in. With one foot after the other we eventually reached our seats just about the time the game started. For good luck, I rubbed the head of the guy sitting directly in front of me. He immediately turned around and spat out a litany of curse words. Obviously, he did not find my gesture humorous. Within a few minutes, security was on the scene. They escorted me to the gates and off of the premises as persona non grata.

I had been kicked out of football games before due to my drinking. This was nothing new. I just took the punishment. Still, I felt embarrassed. The purpose of my trip to Knoxville was to support Ramon and his wife not get kicked out of a game. I roamed around the city for the next few hours until my date caught up with me and helped me sober up. She informed me that the Volunteers beat the Gators 30-6, so I figured that Ramon must have been happy. All I could think about was apologizing to him for not supporting his efforts with Carolina Bedding. Once I returned to Jacksonville, I called him and apologized. He told me not to worry about it and invited me to come up for the next Tennessee game.

I was not only getting kicked out of games, however. I was also getting kicked off of planes. A few weeks before that Tennessee game, a group of us, including my marketing rep, E.S., and several vendors from name brand mattress companies that we worked with, had planned a trip to Bandon, Oregon, a small town on the coast where the Coquille River meets the Pacific. Bandon is known for its nationally ranked golf resort, Bandon Dunes, which is a little north of the city along with Bullard's Beach State Park. The resort offers birds-eye views of the ocean from its green fairways and grass-covered rocky cliffs.

The trips we took, such as this one, were rarely about business but more about socializing. Alcohol was always involved. Some of the people who were attending did not even know my given name. They just called me "Rockstar", a moniker that I was proud of for some reason. It never dawned on me that the nickname was due to my drinking prowess.

The first evening we played two rounds of golf on the Bandon Dunes course. The games were social, not competitive. We played in groups of four. The views from the course were phenomenal and the weather cool and pleasant. I felt as if we were golfing somewhere in the British Isles and that a flock of sheep might stroll across the fairway. The following morning, we decided to play another round on the Pacific Trail course before flying to Portland, Oregon. For the 400-mile-plus trip, we took a small commuter jet upon which we had been served ample amounts of complimentary beer and wine. From Portland, our destination was Las Vegas to attend the furniture market. By the time we reached Portland International Airport, I was intoxicated. I took my seat among the others in the first-class section of the plane. While we were waiting for all of the passengers to board, I decided I would entertain everyone. I got up and grabbed a flashlight from the galley and pretended it was a light saber, much to the dismay of the flight attendant. I begged her not to kick me off of the flight, but she was adamant. Security was called and I was escorted off of the plane and taken to a hotel to sober up. The airline generously rebooked me on a flight to Las Vegas the next morning so the effects of the alcohol would have time to subside. After I was dropped off at the hotel, I tried buying a drink from the bar, but they would not serve me, so I walked to a gas station and bought a six-pack. Back in my hotel room, I flipped a tab and drank half of a can of beer before conking out for the night; that is how intoxicated I was.

The next morning, I thanked God that I was kicked off of that plane because had I made it to Las Vegas, who knows what might have happened. I recognized the gravity of what had happened the day before. My first instincts told me to call E.S. He was my supplier and I wanted to make sure that we were still good. “I can’t believe I did that,” I said apologetically when he picked up the call. He laughed it off and said everything was okay and that he would see me later in the day when I got to Las Vegas. After I landed at the airport, I joined the group and we attended the market, played golf at the TPC Las Vegas, gambled at the casinos, and continued to drink. The types of people that I had attracted into my inner circle were good people, but they were also heavy drinkers so there was no escaping alcohol. Although I felt embarrassed about what had happened, I still failed to see that I had a drinking problem.

When I returned to Florida, I immediately got back into my routine, recruiting by day, and by night, still drinking. There was also Carolina Bedding's company incentive trip to the Caribbean to look forward to, which would be happening within the next few days. About 35 of our dealers would be attending. These were people that I had known for a long time so this trip would also be like a reunion. For some reason, I had decided to bring the same woman, Brittany, with me on the cruise that I had to the Tennessee-Florida game. My mom even offered to help her out by babysitting her children in Ohio for the week that we would be on the cruise.

The first night on the ship, Brittany and I attended the cocktail meet and greet. Things were going well until she said something inappropriate. I took her to the side and whispered in her ear, "Why would you say something like that?" She became angry with me and stormed off. I, on the other hand, was not going to succumb to the drama. I accompanied my friends to the casino to play blackjack. An older couple joined me at the table, and I was teaching the Mrs. how to play when Brittany came into the casino looking for me. She was still angry, most likely because I had not chased after her, and abruptly left the casino in a huff. Like I said earlier, I am a "chill" type of person and am not accustomed to such drama. I excused myself from the couple and went to look for her. Back in the room, she was sitting on the balcony wrapped in a towel. She did not even look up when I entered and continued to ignore me. I saw four shots of Jägermeister on the nightstand. I did not say a word and instead drank them all, to protect her from drinking them herself. I then called the steward, making sure that he saw her sitting on the balcony and me leaving the room.

The next morning, Brittany met us at the pool, not looking very cheery, and somewhat hungover, just like the rest of us were. I ordered a bucket of waters for the group, but my card had been deactivated. I excused myself, walked to the front desk, got the card reinstated, and returned to the pool. While a bunch of us were at the pool just hanging out, one of my friends mentioned that there was going to be a blackjack tournament in a couple of hours. I said I was definitely in. Those tournaments were short and fun. For $40 you get $1,000 worth of chips. You can bet on one hand and double your money, or you can play up to ten hands.

Things were going smoothly at the tournament, until I was suddenly interrupted by one of my friends. Brittany dove into the pool and hit her head on the bottom. She was in the infirmary.

Was she okay, I asked?

Before he could answer, the loudspeaker blared my name.

"Attention, Mr. Darren Conrad. Please report to the captain's office. Attention, Mr. Darren Conrad."

I assumed that the captain wanted to inform me about what had happened to Brittany. I swiftly made my way to his office where his assistant led me to a chair, Here I was seated directly in front of the captain with members of his crew seated on both sides of him. Six of his attendants filed into the room and stood behind me. It felt intense and intimidating.

"Mr. Conrad," the captain said looking me straight in the eye. "You can no longer drink on this ship. We will be deciding whether or not to ask you to disembark this evening and we will let you know our decision tomorrow. We were at sea and would be reaching the Grand Cayman Islands in the morning.

That evening I was not sure what to do. I walked up to the top deck, watching the dark sea roll before me. The stars were twinkling through the few scattered clouds on the dark palette of sky. A couple of my friends joined me on deck. I was nearly in tears, feeling like a dead man walking. I had not even had anything to drink all day, and I certainly was not going to have anything to drink tonight. My friends tried to console me, but I also knew that they probably did not want to stay on deck all night. I told them to go to the casino. They asked me to come with them, but I declined. It felt strange and weird not to be drinking, but I needed to avoid alcohol tonight. Captain's orders!

The next morning, I was hopeful that I would be able to stay on the ship. Shortly after we docked at the Grand Cayman Islands, those hopes were dashed when I was informed that I had to disembark. Everyone attending the incentive cruise was shocked. But the cruise would continue with or without me. My second-hand man, M.H., now the CEO of the company, who had been running Carolina Bedding for some time was still on board.

My date asked to leave the ship with me. I told her, "No, Brittany, you can't. Remember? You did not bring your passport with you. You stay on the ship and enjoy the rest of the cruise." Once I got onshore, I booked a nice four-star hotel for a few days, then took a stroll on the beach to take in what had just happened to me. I ran into the older couple I had met at the casino.

"Aren't you heading the wrong way?" they asked me. I explained what had happened and they were in disbelief.

The cruise line had booked a flight for me back to the U.S. but while I was in Grand Cayman, I planned to have some fun. I went back to the hotel and started drinking, looking for people to hang out with despite just being kicked off of the ship. I connected with some locals, who were partiers, and met some girls from overseas. They took me to a party, a scene which made me rather uncomfortable, so I left. I was continually getting sent signals that it was time to stop drinking. I just was not receiving them. Either that or I was simply ignoring them.

When I returned to Florida, the Ohio State-Michigan game was coming up. I did not want to watch the game at the bar alone, so I called up Tiffany to see if she wanted to meet me. Yes, the wild and crazy Tiffany that I had moved to Jacksonville Beach to avoid. I don't know what compelled me to call her, but I did. She decided to join me.

There was something fun and adventurous about being with another wild and crazy drinker. When she and I were together, I felt like we were Bonnie and Clyde, Harry and Sally, and Samson and Delilah all rolled into one. Hanging out with her was like riding a death-defying roller coaster, but the ride only remained thrilling for so long; it eventually coasted and came to an abrupt stop, or in a worst-case scenario, the coaster fell off the tracks. Being with Tiffany was more like falling off of the tracks.

During the game, we got really drunk at the bar as usual. Afterwards, we got a ride back to my place. When I opened the door and flicked on the light, something just flicked in my brain like that light switch. What was I doing? Was this how I was going to spend my life? I was almost 40 years old, and I needed to start taking responsibility for my behavior. I had to put my drinking behind me. The two of us slept off the alcohol's deleterious effects. In the morning, when

I was able to drive, I took Tiffany home. When I got back, I asked God to help me. Actually, I did not ask Him. I implored Him. I begged Him. I fell on my knees and surrendered to Him. I deleted Tiffany's number from my phone and never contacted or saw her again. Considering my drinking history, that was not a decision that I made lightly.

That morning I did some soul searching. I pulled out my yearbook from junior high school. All of the kids wrote notes in my yearbook. Most of the time they wrote something like, "To Alki." So many other people, even in my younger years, recognized that I had a drinking problem. Except for me! It suddenly hit me. This was the first time I recognized that I was an alcoholic and could see myself like everybody else did. I stayed home and did not drink for three days. On the third day, my pool girl, a sweet, petite, blonde, came over to clean the pool. I walked out onto the pool deck to say hi to her. She looked at me and said, "I have been in recovery for two and one-half years. It changed my life. I go to recovery meetings every week. It's like a fellowship." I had never told her that I drink, but somehow, she knew. I felt as if she was a messenger from God, telling me what I needed to hear when I was wise enough and ready to receive it.

I decided to try sobriety for one year to see how it would feel. Would my life be better? Would I still know how to have fun and enjoy life? If my life improved in one year, I would stay sober. If not, then I would go back to drinking alcohol. This day, November 22, 2008, was the beginning of a new life. I did not realize it at the time, but that was the day I truly started growing and living. It was the day that I realized I did indeed have a drinking problem.

PART III

Clean Slate

Chapter Sixteen

On April 1, 2009, I checked my mailbox and found a strange-looking envelope bulging at the seams. Oddly, it had been addressed to me by hand. An attorney's address was on the return. Was this a joke? I had quite a few friends who knew I had legal troubles, and I would not put it past them to try to trick me on April Fool's Day.

As I opened the envelope, I realized this was not a joke but a legal document with serious implications: A summary judgement for $650,000, including damages and legal fees, allegedly for violating a non-compete agreement with PMD. The judgement said I could no longer own nor run my mattress company, Carolina Bedding, a successful business I had created and built after I had left PMD and moved to South Carolina with my first wife Melanie and her children.

Coupled with my federal tax bill, I was in debt to the amount of $1,000,000.00. That was too many zeros following that big "one" for me! My stomach muscles instantly tensed up and my nerves felt like I had just received an electrical shock. Not only was the amount I owed painful, what was more painful was that I had to give up Carolina Bedding. If this were a joke, it would have been the cruelest kind.

My mission now was to save Carolina Bedding and not leave the dealers stranded. There was only one way I could accomplish this. I rounded up M. H., Shannon, and Dan on a conference call to break the news. They, too, were in shock! I told them not to worry, that Carolina Bedding would stay in business and that I would be equally dividing the company among the three of them. As these words tumbled out of my mouth, I felt like King Lear, the unstable Shakespearean king who divided his kingdom among his three daughters in an attempt to find out which one loved him the most. Like Lear, I had three dealers who had helped me run the company. But would they be loyal and true? M.H. had been my number one for some time now. He had been one of my first Carolina Bedding customers, who quickly became a successful dealer, so much so that I made him president of the company. Shannon and Dan, the two others who would receive a slice of the three-piece pie, were loyal friends and co-workers, people I trusted would be good to the dealers. Here I was dividing up my kingdom and giving it away before my time had come.

As in all Shakespearean tragedies, the protagonist commits a fatal flaw. Sometimes this flaw has to do with hubris, pride, or ego. My fatal flaw had to do with the ability, or lack thereof, to let go. A couple of years back, E.S., my manufacturing rep, had offered to pay me my percentage directly, which I felt at the time would bypass my involvement with my dealers. I declined at first but then later took him up on his offer because I found myself spending a lot of time chasing bouncing checks and receiving late payments. The previous arrangement called for the dealers to email me a spreadsheet with their orders, which I would keep track of on a dry erase board, probably not the most efficient of systems. I was constantly dealing with money, to the sum of $30,000 to $60,000 in orders per week. E.S. set it up so that the dealers would order directly from him, and I would be paid a rebate for my services.

At the time I received this judgement against me, I could have turned to drinking, but I did the opposite. I continued to lean on my sobriety. I was already committed to staying sober, having completed five solid months of recovery. Unlike the time I attended recovery meetings upon my divorce from Melanie, this time I wanted to discover what it would be like to be sober. This time I made myself a promise that I would evolve into a better person. I attended meetings seven days a week, sometimes two or three times a day, while running Carolina Bedding. My goal had been to meet as many recovering or recovered alcoholics as possible in order to see how they were now living a sober life and if they were feeling happy and fulfilled.

At my first meeting, I met a young man named Jim who offered to be my temporary sponsor. He made a huge impact on my recovery. Together, we started working through the 12 steps. The first step was that I had to admit that I was powerless over alcohol and that my life had become unmanageable. By taking this first step, I had surrendered.

Before Melanie and I had divorced, and before I found out she had been embezzling money from the company, she was in charge of the administrative and financial part of the business. She was very good at helping in that arena so that I could focus on recruiting and training. When we divorced in 2005, I assumed that she had filed the company's taxes, but I later learned that she did not. For the next several years, I held the mistaken belief that if I had not filed and paid my taxes for 2005, then I could not file my taxes for 2006. Four years went by, and I still had not filed or paid my federal taxes. As soon as I received a check in the mail, I would cash it, then put the money in a safe. I had so many cash bills that I would wrap them into stacks. Eventually, I had acquired more than $100,000. The practice of locking money up became a survival tactic, but that tactic had also become a burden. I knew that the money I was stashing was not truly mine because I owed it. Having it in my possession felt uncomfortable because I did not feel like a legitimate tax-paying citizen. Like a dark cloud over my head, I maintained an underlying fear of the IRS. This manner of living in constant fear and strife contributed to my drinking habit, which continued to spiral out of control.

When I made the decision to become sober and took those first steps to achieve my goal, I realized that part of my recovery would involve making amends. I had to fix things that were broken, and my federal income taxes were certainly broken. I picked up the phone and called the IRS. When they answered, I said, "Hey, I haven't paid my income tax for the last four years and I'd like to pay them." I was a nervous wreck when I made that call, but the person on the other end of the line was kind, calm, and reassuring. She helped me set up a plan to pay my back taxes, and with additional help from a retired accountant named Sam Brown that I had met through a friend, I was able to start making payments on my tax bill, which was around $350,000. Cleaning the slate with the IRS was one of the things that helped me achieve sobriety.

Even though I could not work in the mattress industry for one year, and my main focus was staying sober, my mind was continually thinking about ways to make the mattress business bigger, faster, and stronger than ever before. During that year I met quite a few people who tried to get me involved in MLM businesses, but I had never been a fan of that type of business plan. The products they sold never seemed any more superior to what could be purchased through public means. I just did not believe in pushing a product that I did not believe in. And, for me, believing in the product is vital to a business. In addition, I still firmly held the belief that establishing a brick-and-mortar business, a business with a physical address that a person would be proud to call their own, and making money as well as offering a great product, is more meaningful. There was one thing that had inspired me, however, about MLM businesses—their presentations and their promotional videos. I focused my efforts on creating an informational and inspirational video about the company that could be used during the recruiting process. I drafted a compelling script and hired a videographer to create a video that would bring everything together.

In September of my year away from the business, even though I was not in any way involved with Carolina Bedding, I attended the company's incentive trip to Aruba. This allowed me to keep in touch with everybody on a friendly level, not a corporate one. It was a small crew that year. M.H. attended with his wife and his daughter and her soon-to-be husband. I knew them all well and felt as if I was taking a trip with my family. The trip, although it only lasted for four days, was also life-changing because it was my first sober trip to the Caribbean. It was as if I had been blind, and now I could see; the dark lenses of alcoholism had been lifted. The crystal blue waters looked so clear and so beautiful. I enjoyed snorkeling, windsurfing, boating, and fishing more than I ever had during my entire life. In the evening, I supped on delicious dinners without alcohol and the next morning, it was a joy to wake up, not feeling hungover or wondering what I had done the night before, or how much money I had spent, or worse. Shortly after we returned from Aruba, I invited M.H. to Columbus to go to an OSU Buckeyes' football game and to visit my family's farm where we had a bonfire.

Another April Fool's Day came and went, and I was now legally allowed to participate in the mattress business once again. I felt it was time to return to Carolina Bedding, but this time it would be in a different capacity. I would serve as a consultant to help grow and develop the company. The year I had been away Carolina Bedding had not flourished, in my opinion, as it should have. Dan and Shannon had left their positions with the company, leaving M.H. as sole ruler of the kingdom. One of the first things I did upon my return was meet with M.H. and his leadership team, several of them whom I did not personally know, in Cancun, Mexico, to put a plan into action to launch the company big time. Several months later, in August 2010, I attended the company's incentive trip, which took place that year on an Alaskan cruise. It was then that I made the decision to leave Jacksonville Beach and move to Charlotte, North Carolina, to create a corporate headquarters and a training center for Carolina Bedding.

On October 2, 2010, I moved to Charlotte, where I rented a condo at The Ivey's, an old department store that had been renovated into luxury condominium units, complete with restaurants and an athletic complex within walking distance. As soon as I settled in, I started attending recovery meetings and concentrated on building a recovery fellowship as a support system. I met a wonderful lady named Suzy at the gym. She was into fitness, like me, and seemed to be living a healthy lifestyle. She was very beautiful, and I was immediately attracted to her. One of the first things I told her was, "I live a sober life. I don't drink." I wanted to impress upon her the fact that maintaining my sobriety was important to me. She expressed that she rarely drank, only some wine occasionally in the evenings. I was okay with that. I did not want alcohol to dictate whom I should or should not be dating. We continued spending time together, yet I was fighting with myself. "I can do this," I would tell myself. "I don't need to listen to the suggestions made in my recovery meetings. I can be with people who drink and not drink myself." Despite my inner battle, Suzy and I highly enjoyed each other's company, whether we were going out to dinner, working out, or attending many of Charlotte's offerings. After a short while, we became engaged. She rented the home she owned in Charlotte so we could move into a larger home, big enough for us and her three school-aged children, big enough for me to have my own office and library.

When I had set sail on that Alaskan cruise the past fall, I was impressed with the pristine beauty of our northernmost state. Traversing the glacial waters surrounding the rocky snow-covered mountains and stopping off at port towns that were barely a dot on the map, was surreal. This was rugged, untouched country. So, when Suzy mentioned that she had family in Anchorage, we planned a family vacation with her kids for the month of July. I was looking forward to going on a land-based adventure and to meeting her extended family. On our to-do list was visiting the borough of Telkeetna, the southern gateway to the Mt. Denali basecamp, with a population of less than one thousand and an average high July temperature of less than 70 degrees. I had seen a *Man vs. Food* episode that took place at the Talkeetna Roadhouse and wanted to make sure we all had a meal together there. We also visited Homer, a small city on Kachemak Bay on the Kenai peninsula, a 200-mile drive south of Anchorage via AK-1, which traced the coastline offering panoramic mountain views and mirrored images of the mountains in the frigid waters below them. I caught salmon on the Kenai River, which is the best place to catch them in the world according to locals. This trip was the pinnacle of our relationship. Yet it was also the beginning of its downfall. When visiting with her family members, I saw a different side of Suzy. I was not comfortable with their behavior as a group, but I pretended to be. I no longer enjoyed being around people who were drunk, although since becoming sober, I have had to at various work functions. In those situations, I can just get up and leave. But this was Suzy, my partner, the woman who was supposed to be my ally, and I, hers. It is not that I wanted or needed her to change her behavior, but I could not just sit back and say, *"You guys go out and drink, but it's not my thing."* The trip changed the dynamic of our relationship, but I was still hopeful that things would work out.

By this time, I had been sober for three years. I had learned a lot about alcoholism by working on my own recovery and sobriety. Through the programs I was attending and through my mentors, I learned that alcoholism is not about drinking alcohol. Alcohol is merely a solution to an underlying spiritual problem. Alcoholics, in general, are extremely self-centered, selfish to the core, and all of their decisions are based upon "self." Left untreated, the disease of alcoholism results in a miserable living existence. People can become addicted to anything. Some people become addicted to food. Others to shopping or gambling. Alcoholism is more common than you would think, and it stems from a lack of having God in your life. Spiritually, the alcoholic may think things, such as "I don't feel good enough," "I don't feel confident," or "I like to drink because it breaks the barriers so I can do something." Physically, an alcoholic has what is similar to an allergic reaction in the way the body metabolizes or breaks down alcohol. The body craves more and more and more alcohol. There is no stop button. The alcoholic has no gauge. There is no middle ground. There are only two temperatures: Kenya and Antarctica. Having a beer with a burger makes no sense to me. Not even drinking a six-pack makes sense to me. A twelve-pack? Yes, that makes sense. This is the mindset of the alcoholic, which is rooted in excess.

During this time of my life, business was still booming. But it is one thing when you are working closely with someone who lives in another city and another thing when you are actually living in the same city. M.H. and I also saw things differently. He wanted to focus on the furniture side of the business to include outdoor patio furniture, dining room and living room sets. I, however, fervently believed that the mattress side of the business was crucial for success. Some of our dealers sold furniture in addition to mattresses, but the mattress side of the business was the backbone. He was also interested in starting a kitchen cabinet business. Together, we travelled to Cleveland, Ohio, to look at potential kitchen cabinet business models, but after attending the presentation, we both decided that was not the path we wanted Carolina Bedding to take. While we were in Cleveland, M.H. acted in ways that would derail me from my commitment to sobriety, which is something a good friend would not do. Later on, I learned from another source that he had started a kitchen cabinet business on his own, not that it was an issue for me, but the fact that he kept it secretive eroded the trust I had in him.

Despite the red flags, I continued growing Carolina Bedding using the recruiting methods I had developed over the years, the training manual I had written, and my advertising techniques which I deemed as proprietary. I was doing everything I could to help the business evolve while M.H. was collecting the checks. It did not help matters that he took the larger office at the warehouse we were leasing, and that I was relegated to the small closet, literally. After one year of working as a consultant, I realized that it was time to talk to him. It was a simple conversation. I wanted to become part owner of the company. He said he would think about it. He gave me his answer the next day when he changed the locks on the doors of the headquarters building and left my belongings (mainly photos and books) on the doorstep in a cardboard box with a note attached that said, "Good luck." He also called our sales rep, E.S., and told him to stop sending me my rebate checks. That day, October 7, 2011, seemed to be the day the fatal flaw in my tale had become manifest.

With my belongings on the doorstep, I looked at my watch. I still had a training session to conduct in an hour. Being the company's only trainer, I did not want to dodge my responsibility to the dealers. I spent the entire day training the new dealers as well as the returning ones. As I spoke to the group, I pretended not to notice M.H. and his leadership team sitting in the back of the room. I played it cool, acting as if I did not know that I had been kicked out of the company. Obviously, he did not realize that I had already received his answer! After I finished teaching the training session that day, I left the room without saying goodbye to anyone. I just walked down the hallway, listening to the chatter of the dealers about the upcoming dinner that night. "Hey, where's Darren going?" someone asked. "I think he's going to deliver a mattress or something," another voice answered. I kept walking, smiling to myself, never looking back.

Chapter Seventeen

The day I got locked out of Carolina Bedding headquarters turned out to be one of the best days of my life. I was now free to move forward in a more positive direction. No matter how much you give someone or something the benefit of a doubt, no matter how many red flags you chose to ignore, the negative people and things in your life will eventually fade away if you remain positive and true to your calling. On the surface, being turned down for a partnership with Carolina Bedding might have seemed like an ominous turn of events, but M.H. letting me go made me want to start all over again. The fact that I now had zero income also fueled my fire to build something new. One week after getting kicked out of Carolina Bedding, on October 11, 2011, I started another mattress company, Carolina Bedding Direct.

It is not only the protagonist of a story that can make a fatal flaw, however; an antagonist can make one, too. M.H. was good at running a business. He was intelligent and he was motivated. But he did not realize the value of creating and maintaining relationships. He most certainly did not recognize the value of the relationships I had formed with the

Carolina Bedding dealers. When I started Carolina Bedding Direct, 30 Carolina Bedding dealers followed me, including a new dealer named Kyle Sherratt, whom I had met during that last training session I had just given. Kyle was bright, sharp, creative, and motivated, certainly the type of person I wanted to be a part of my new company.

M. H. was obviously not happy that so many of the Carolina Bedding dealers left his company to follow me. Lawsuits were filed against those dealers, but they were settled rather quickly and in a positive manner. I had hired an attorney to represent all of them. Our main defense was that I was the original owner of Carolina Bedding, not M.H. This meant that the noncompete agreements they signed were with me, not him. The court also allowed me to retain my recruiting video, my promotional video of the business model, and, most importantly, the name Carolina Bedding Direct.

Sam Brown, the retired accountant who was instrumental in helping me manage my IRS debt as well as my finances, was excited about the prospects my new company would bring. He offered to help me work out the legal details. Sam was an impressive person. Intelligent, sharp, and shrewd. He had previously worked for a well-known and prestigious accounting firm, so I trusted his advice and made him my accountant. I also decided to continue working with E.S., Carolina Bedding's mattress sales rep., because he was now working as a sales rep for a major bedding manufacturer. This was definitely a plus! The company he now worked for had the capability to deliver mattresses throughout the country, which meant Carolina Bedding Direct would not be geographically limited like Carolina Bedding had been. Working with E.S. in this new capacity felt like a move in the right direction. As a result of this decision, we quickly increased the number of Carolina Bedding Direct locations.

One of the things I did differently with Carolina Bedding Direct was to hire an IT guy to create a company website with automated systems. I believe that systems build and run companies, not people. Potential dealers could now go to the website to sign up, sign the confidentiality agreement and complete other paperwork, and participate in our training sessions. The website also featured a real-time leaderboard with the top dealers. It was an interactive and dynamic system, an online space accessible by all that emanated positivity and professionalism. We now had one unified place, an automated, one-stop-shop, where dealers could go to place their orders, sign their agreements, and be recognized, educated, and inspired!

Another thing I did differently with Carolina Bedding Direct was set up an amazing ad system which was deployed on various online platforms. It was a simple system, yet it did the trick! When a prospective candidate answered the ad, I scheduled an interview with them. It was that simple. That is how I met a charismatic man, D.D. His professional sales background included MLM companies and various franchises. D.D. was a dynamic speaker with the draw of an evangelical preacher. He was hungry for success and had a personality that lit up a room. Every Monday, he handled our national calls, his goal always to get as many people on those calls as he could. Being the electric speaker that he was, he would get 200 to 300 people on each of those calls. His personality encompassed enthusiasm and exuded positive energy. We did not need to sell. Our business was an attraction, not a promotion. With D.D. on board, the floodgates had been opened and because of his success and growth, I made him the president of the company.

D.D.'s approach always included strong views surrounding his Christian beliefs. Thus, his words could be motivational, but they could also be chastising. I was not always comfortable with this because I did not want to bring religion into the company. I felt that people's beliefs are personal, and that religion and business should remain separate. D.D., however, had this unbelievable energy that attracted people. They wanted to be on the call with him. They wanted to hear him speak. They were moved by his energy. Still, people either liked D.D. or they did not. My sales rep E.S. fell into that latter category. It seemed to me that he had gravitated to my accountant Sam Brown, perhaps, to wedge his way deeper into the company. In looking back, I suspect that E.S. may have put a bug in Sam's ear along the lines of, "Darren can be emotional and not always make the best decisions," as if he were trying to save me from myself. A casual conversation I had with Sam heightened those suspicions. One more than one occasion, he suggested that it might be better for me to own 55 percent of a larger company than to be the sole owner of a smaller company. He also said that it might also be in my best interest to form a partnership with E.S. instead of D.D. This put me in an awkward position. If I sided with D.D., whom most people liked, I might also lose Sam, a valuable asset to the company. I highly trusted Sam, perhaps more so than anyone else in the company. He was a highly respectable man and wise for his years.

Despite the company's success, I was becoming depressed. Losing Carolina Bedding had been like a hit out of left field. I also realized that I was in a serious relationship with a major drinker. This came to a head on St. Patrick's Day 2012. My fiancée Suzy decided at the last minute to take a girls-only trip to Savannah, Georgia. Now, Savannah's celebration is always held on the actual day drawing large crowds and involving copious amounts of drinking and partying. I agreed to watch Suzy's kids while she was away. They were school age and old enough to take care of themselves, so I was not babysitting, just supervising. During Suzy's trip, I made numerous attempts to reach her, but she never picked up her phone. I left messages but she never returned them. What could she possibly be doing? My mind was doing mental and emotional gymnastics trying to figure it out. I know what I would have been doing if I was on an all-buddies St. Patrick's Day party during my drinking years, and that would not be something good. When Suzy returned, she saw that I was down and thought I might be homesick. Maybe I should take a trip home back to Jacksonville Beach and go to the ocean, she suggested. I did not take much time to think about her suggestion. Within the hour I was driving back to Florida.

Once I got to Jacksonville Beach, I booked a room at the Quality Suites on the ocean and took a stroll on the beach. The smell of the salt air and the warming rays of the sun made me feel better. The sound of the waves crashing on the shore as I lay in bed that night soothed and calmed me. I woke early feeling refreshed. After breakfast, I drove to Ponte Vedra Beach to attend a men's recovery meeting, one that I had frequented when I previously lived here. When I walked into the room, I was surprised that I recognized everyone. Although I did not know each man personally or by name, in the grand scheme of things, it did not matter. There was more value to me in not having a verbal connection. It was more about just being there. Being together. The dark mask of depression, worry, and anxiety that I had been wearing as of late had been lifted. I immediately felt welcome, safe, and comfortable, like I had just come back home. *This is where you need to be*, I thought. *You are in the right place*. I was now here, a part of this kinship, this tight-knit community.

The next day was a beautiful Sunday morning. I made the decision to drive to Jacksonville Beach to attend a coed meeting. Coinciding with the recovery meeting was a social. There I saw a beautiful, slender, blonde woman who immediately caught my eye. She was beaming, like a glowing angel. I was too afraid to approach her directly. Alcoholics have a fear of rejection, and I certainly did. We can act grandiose and at the same time have an inferiority complex, which is quite an oxymoron in itself. I asked someone what her name was and found out that it was "Chloe," an unusual name. I looked her up on Facebook and saw that we had 30 friends in common, but it took me one month to send her a friend request. She accepted my request a few days later. I then messaged her, asking if she wanted to meet for coffee. When she did not respond, I wrote, "Forget coffee. Dinner." Two days later I still had not heard anything and felt rejected. To my surprise, she responded with a note that said, yes, she would like to get together.

I never did return to Charlotte. Instead, I moved back into my old place at the Metropolitan, the condo where I had been living before moving to North Carolina. Shortly thereafter, Suzy drove to Florida to bring my few belongings. I thanked her and we said our goodbyes. After Chloe's and my first date, we started spending more and more time together. We enjoyed each other's company even though we were polar opposites. We had been dating for several months when I received the tragic news that my younger brother Dan had passed away. Chloe was supportive and naturally blended into my family. Having known her for only a few months, I asked her to marry me, and she said yes. We both wanted to have a beautiful, well-planned ceremony and reception, so we set a date.

A few months before the wedding, I offered E.S. 45 percent ownership of the company for $100,000, and he agreed. The funds would certainly help me pay for the wedding but that was not the reason I asked him to become a partner. It had taken me a year to consider Sam's advice. The company needed a president who could be neutral, and it appeared to me at the time that E.S. was more valuable in that respect. We now had a board of directors, and the name of the company, at E.S.'s behest, was changed to Mattress by Appointment, which was more indicative of how we did business. With E.S. as president, Darren left to form his own company and took some of the dealers with him. E.S. sued Darren, a decision with which I did not agree. The lawsuit created friction between us because I knew that Darren was a good guy, even though he might not have been the best choice in the long run as president of the company. By now, our accountant Sam Brown was not as excited about the business as he had originally been. He was now in his retirement years and was enjoying spending time with his young grandchildren. With the company's operations now being run from Florida, he suggested I find a Florida-based accountant.

Not long after E.S. came on board as part-owner, Chloe and I got married. The wedding took place at the Lodge and Club at Ponte Vedra Beach with about 150 guests in attendance. She looked simply stunning in her ivory dress and tiara. I felt awed upon seeing her, my beautiful wife. For the occasion I wore a bespoke tuxedo, a blue Daniel Craig-James Bond style with a hand-tied bow tie. Liz Stewart Floral design created the elegant floral arrangements for both our wedding and the reception. Cinotti's Bakery created a masterpiece of a wedding cake that looked too beautiful to eat. The Cloud 9 band played the music at our reception. I even took dance lessons so I would be prepared to dance to our song, Eric Clapton's,

Wonderful Tonight. It was such a special day, and we were very happy.

For our honeymoon, I had researched the top 20 resorts in the Caribbean and chose Jade Mountain Resort in St. Lucia. The week we stayed there felt as if we had escaped into our own private sanctuary. From the airport, we were driven on a dirt road that snaked up and down the mountains, completely surrounded by lush forest and the sound of gentle waves beyond the trees. Our room had a view of the sea surrounded by emerald pyramid-shaped mountains that pierced the Caribbean sky. We spent the days strolling and swimming on our own private beach. While we were at the resort, we saw no one there, other than our steward. I felt as if Chloe and I were the only woman and man in the world.

To begin our married life, I had wanted to rent a quaint three-bedroom home with a guest house on Atlantic Beach, but due to my credit, I had been rejected. My parents drove down to the house and bought it for us as a wedding gift from both them and my brothers. I had never asked for anything financially from my parents. We were shocked, awed, and touched by their gift.

While we were away, it seemed as if E.S. took this as an opportunity to start making allegations against me to the board of directors. When I returned from my honeymoon, Brandon, my new accountant, pulled me aside and told me that I should pay E.S. back. I had no idea what Brandon was talking about and asked him to clarify what expenses he was referring to. Through various company receipts, I was able to show Brandon that I did not owe E.S. any money. At the next board meeting, I confronted E.S. in front of everyone and asked him to justify his claims. He could not provide any evidence. The board dismissed him as president, but he still owned 45 percent of the company. He filed a lawsuit against me to buy him out of his shares within 60 days. That request was impossible due to my financial situation. My bank accounts had been drained when Scott Andrew had been awarded PMD in a lawsuit resulting in the $650,000 judgement against me.

E.S. did not give up. He offered me $3 million dollars for my 55 percent share of the company, which could easily have paid off the judgement, but I ignored the offer. I just could not put my dealers under his leadership after the false allegations he had made against me. In an attempt to save Mattress by Appointment, I consulted an accounting firm for options. They recommended I file for Chapter 7 bankruptcy because the Mattress By Appointment did not own any financial assets. The company did not own any buildings, nor did it own any inventory. The company's only asset was me and my knowledge. This was confirmed when I interviewed with the bankruptcy court. In a bankruptcy trust, however, the officers are often highly motivated to collect because they receive a percentage of any monies or assets gained. E.S. worked a deal through his attorneys to pay the remainder of my $650,000 judgement to RSS, thus buying me out my shares of Mattress By Appointment in bankruptcy. Had I played the wrong hand? It might have seemed so because I lost Mattress By Appointment. The result of all of this, however, was that I was now debt free! The massive amount of debt from the judgement had been wiped away. Instead of being upset about this, I felt humbled. The most difficult challenges in my life have always turned out to be blessings, blessings which have always given me a clean slate allowing me to begin again.

PART IV

The Rugged Road Trip

Chapter Eighteen

The city of Port St. Lucie lies on Florida's Treasure Coast and is the third largest metropolis in south Florida, surpassing the population of even Fort Lauderdale. While travelling on the interstate, I have passed the city many times but have never stopped by or paid it much notice. In the winter of 2019, after I had docked at the Fort Lauderdale Port from going on the Buckeye Cruise for Cancer, I decided to visit Port St. Lucie on my way back to Jacksonville Beach. Once I exited, I saw at first glance that the city was low-key, beautiful, and serene.

There was a reason I was stopping here: To greet the owners of a new BoxDrop® location in the area. When I walked into their store, John and Brenda's faces lit up. They were more than welcoming upon my arrival, showing me around, telling me about their successes, and asking me how they might sustain that success. They appreciated the time I took to stop by, check in, and see how things were going on a more personal level. The visit was a reminder of the power of face-to-face connection.

It had been nearly two years since I had become Executive Vice President and Chief Marketing Officer (CMO) of Retail

Service Systems, Inc. (RSS). It took a bit of humility to step down as CEO of Mattress Direct, even though I did not have a choice. In 2015 and 2016, I had been helping RSS, all the while still entangled in what seemed to be a spider's web of legal disputes. I remained positive throughout it all, and, with goodwill, I travelled throughout the country educating RSS dealers about the systems I had created and sharpened during my 20 years of building and creating various mattress companies. Yes, I had given RSS my plan, treating and interacting with the company as if it were my own business, even though I was not on the payroll. The only way I can explain my actions is that I had an innate faith that I would be an owner of RSS one day. That did happen two years later after the fierce legal battle I had been fighting had finally come to an end. Along with the end of this legal battle, the 60-day jail sentence I had been ordered to serve was also dismissed. I was ecstatic about finally being able to come back home to Florida and teaming with RSS.

Throughout the years, whether I was consulting for others, or starting my own businesses and building them up or sadly leaving them behind due to lawsuits, I have always continued working on perfecting my simple business model by breaking it down to its smallest elements. Consider how chemists or physicists have determined the structure of living and nonliving organisms by breaking them down to their most basic parts, such as molecules, which are made up of atoms, which, in turn, are composed of electrons, protons, and neutrons, and perhaps even smaller particles than those. My business model is so simple that the modern eye does not always detect it, but it underlies each and every BoxDrop® location—nine beds and a rectangle—whether it is a basic operation or a giant superstore. This simple model has launched the growth of BoxDrop® in 2018 and beyond.

RSS is currently an Inc. 5,000 fast-growing American company and a parent company to two franchises, BoxDrop® and bioPURE™. I gave my 20 years of knowledge and experience in creating systems to help RSS's BoxDrop® franchise succeed, even when I was not sure that I would be a part of the RSS team. I just had faith that things would work out for the best. When I "let go" of being CEO of my own companies and became a part of the RSS team, I found myself in a position where I could travel and connect with people. Sometimes we hold on to a sinking ship thinking that is what will keep us afloat. But when we surrender what we "think" we need, we find our true path. I am now doing what I enjoy and that is what makes me happy. I enjoy interacting with people and helping them succeed. I am not a corporate guy. Scott and Jerry always put the customer first and create ways to help the dealers. Because of this, BoxDrop® offers a stable, sustainable business model that can be followed for the entire life of the business, allowing people to spend more time with their friends and families, ultimately changing the dynamic of their lives.

Jack, the original owner of PMD, seemed strict and rigid to me. Unbendable. It was his way or no way. It is interesting to me how things come full circle. How RSS acquired PMD to make it what it is today and what it should have always been. At RSS, we provide people with a platform and if they wish to become a full retail outlet, then they can. Our mission is to empower rugged entrepreneurs. If they want to sell sofas and dining rooms, that is great. If they want to sell mattresses by appointment, then they can do that too. The model works in various scenarios. If dealers want more income, if they want greater volume, if they want to work more hours and have less flexibility, or if they want more of a life balance, then we support them wherever they are.

I have been in this business for so long that I sometimes forget how unique it is. Twenty years ago, I was not in the mattress business. I was not in the retail store business. I would buy and resell the mattresses for more than I paid for them. I was able to create a system of urgency, offering a great product at a great price, saving the consumer money. I was able to make a good profit selling to many people for a low price with low overhead. I still teach these fundamentals to our dealers. For those who want to evolve and have a retail store operation, we are there to assist as well. But we can always default to the simple, basic system. This is what separates us from other companies.

When I started working for RSS in an official capacity, one of the first things I did was attend the national conference, a four-day cruise to the Bahamas along with about 100 dealers and their spouses. Each year, the company schedules two national trips, one in September and the other in January. These trips provide a way for new dealers to meet the more experienced and successful ones, as well as to provide an opportunity for dealers to engage with leadership in a casual and festive atmosphere. The goal of these trips is to help everyone feel as if they are part of a family. During this specific cruise, I was not only able to reconnect with my previous Mattress Direct dealers and the former PMD dealers, but I was also able to connect with the new RSS folks.

Several months later, in early 2018, I also attended RSS's national trip to the Caribbean Mexico. This trip was monumental because my parents were in attendance. My parents are always engaged in their work and rarely travel, let alone travel outside of the country. Yet here they were finally able to see firsthand what I do in "real-time." As I was spending time with my parents, dealers would approach me and begin a conversation or thank me for helping them succeed. This was the first time I believe my parents realized the significance of my role with RSS. They expressed how proud they were of me. It felt flattering, and their remarks made me blush.

Now, in between those national trips, I continued to do what I had been doing all along: Travelling around the country teaching dealers our simple model and how to use it. My goal was not to try and change the way the dealers were doing business. My goal was to educate them about the system and to create awareness about how powerful it can be. These informal training sessions eventually evolved into what RSS calls their "See America Training." Interestingly, these training sessions did not involve much training, per se. It's not like we were sitting in a classroom teaching math or English. These sessions were about the model. Some of those first meetings had only 30 or 40 people in attendance, which included dealers, their spouses, their managers, and their workers. Over the years, the number of attendees reached into the 100's or more. Seattle, Phoenix, Boston, Tampa, Atlanta, and Columbus, to name several cities, were some of the places where we held these trainings. Dealers, both new and experienced, saw the value in the See America Training events and scheduled them into their business plans. Some dealers attended multiple events each year.

Community-building is tantamount to the success of the training sessions, in addition to creating dealer confidence. As examples, when we held a training session in Salt Lake City, for example, we would also schedule a mountain biking trip, or, if the training were held in winter, we would attend the Sundance Film Festival and go skiing or snowmobiling. In San Francisco, we rented the famous restaurant Pier 65 and also included an excursion to the Golden Gate Bridge.

In New Orleans, we rented busses to chauffeur our dealers to the well-known street party and handed out Mardi Gras beads to everyone. We also dined at some of the French Quarter's old, historic restaurants. These trainings were not only informative, but they were also fun, and they kept the dealers wanting for more, resulting in energy levels that skyrocketed, creating even more excitement for the dealers about their businesses.

So, after that visit to John and Brenda's store in Port St. Lucie, I recognized the great value of one-on-one interactions with the dealers. I shared this insight with both Jerry and Scott and told them about my idea to take yet another road trip across the country, this time with the purpose of visiting as many BoxDrop® dealers as I could along the way. This trip became the company's official "Rugged Road Trip," named after RSS's tag name, "Rugged Entrepreneur." Scott and Jerry suggested that I take two weeks to visit 30 dealers. But I had larger aspirations than that. I was aiming for 100 dealer visits!

Before I left on my trip, I knew that I could not visit the dealers empty-handed. So, I packed "Rugged Entrepreneur" t-shirts and hats into the back of a Chevy Tahoe I had rented, between my luggage, blankets, pillows, and drinks and snacks. Then, at the last minute, my girlfriend Grace called and said that she would like to come along for the ride. She was at my house within the hour! With the van packed to the brim, we left Florida on June 15th, giving us ample time to traverse the east coast before heading to my parents' cabin in Bellaire, Michigan, for the Fourth of July holiday.

My preliminary plan was to follow I-95, from Florida to Maine, stopping at the most successful BoxDrop® dealers that were available for a visit. Along the way, I would call the dealers, tell them I was in the area, and ask if we could set up an impromptu meeting. One of the first dealers we met was located in Augusta, Georgia, who gave us a vintage metal Route 66 road and told us to ask every dealer we met to sign it. At the time, I did not realize how iconic this sign would become as it now sits in our corporate office today. After we left Georgia and began to cover more ground, I realized that the new dealers would also benefit from a personal visit.

I accessed the Roadtrippers App to change the route. Baltimore had originally been our third stop but now it would become the eighth stop as we zigzagged through the Carolinas and Virginia before arriving there to meet with a dealer for dinner. We decided to stop in Washington D.C. first, however, because we wanted to do some sight-seeing. Instead of driving an SUV through the crowded streets of the nation's capital, it seemed like a more practical and fun option for us to rent bikes. At the time, Grace had been suffering from sciatica, so it was much easier for her to ride a bike than walk. We spent the afternoon riding to the Lincoln Memorial, the war memorials, the Washington Monument, the Mall with the museums of the Smithsonian, and, finally, the Capitol Building. It gave me great pause to be at the center of our country, spreading hope and a good message to those following the American Dream that, yes indeed, it can be attainable. I felt as if I was living the American Dream myself, and today, I still do! I was and still am doing what I love, and I love sharing that passion with others. After visiting Baltimore, we headed to Boston, where we rented bikes once again to tour the historical Freedom Trail®. We decided to skip Maine and head west instead.

My goal was to meet with 100 dealers on this trip. On any specific day, I would meet anywhere from three to five dealers. I became so competitive with my own goals that the trip started feeling like a race. I timed the visits to one-half hour, just long enough to meet the dealers, give them a Rugged Entrepreneur t-shirt and hat, have them sign the Route 66 sign, snap a photo, and record a video testimonial. Outside of that, the trip in itself was spontaneous. Grace and I would stop for breakfast or dinner at little, out-of-the-way roadside spots, and look for little wayside hotels as the sun set and the roads darkened for the night.

It was already becoming dark when the dealer and his wife that we visited in Buffalo, New York, suggested we travel to Niagara Falls. The American side was certainly nice, but the better views were observed from the Canadian side. We decided to stay the night and see the falls in the morning. Since neither of us had brought our passports, we decided to take a 15-minute helicopter ride to view the falls after breakfast.

We arrived at my parents' cabin in Bellaire, Michigan, on June 30th and spent five days with them. It was a little break in the middle of such a long and adventurous road trip. My parents liked Grace and we had a great time as usual, cooking out and setting off fireworks. From there, we curved around Lake Michigan and stopped in Minneapolis. That was when our proverbial train derailed. I had to book a hotel for Grace for three nights there because she was waiting to receive a prescription in the mail and needed an address. While she stayed at the hotel, I visited the neighboring dealers, and when I returned, she was no longer blonde but a brunette. Now, that may seem trivial to some, but she gave me no warning and I needed time to get used to her change in appearance. But it was not just her appearance that changed. It was also her demeanor. When my girlfriend and I had first embarked on this trip, I felt as if we were completely in sync. But now, it started to feel as if she was more interested in spending time alone with me and making this trip more about her than the dealers. I was on a work trip, and she had asked to accompany me. Trying to maintain a balancing act by keeping her happy while also keeping my focus on the dealers started to become exhausting. She also began exhibiting some indications of paranoia. Every time I received a phone call or text, I had to explain who was contacting me. In order to alleviate her fears, I would smile and point to the diamond ring on her finger which I had bought her in May.

As we visited dealers along the way, we continued to take small excursions throughout places like Yellowstone, Yosemite, Big Sur, Canyon Lakes, the Arches, Carter Lake, as well as other national parks, experiencing the beautiful scenery and wildlife. There were certain dealers, however, that Grace felt uneasy about us visiting, in particular, certain women. In fact, there was one dealer I had never met in person that I had to skip meeting entirely. Grace had abruptly taken off her ring and asked me to fly her back to Florida unless I cancelled the visit, so I decided not to meet with her. How I wish though that I would have taken Grace up on her offer to fly back home. Instead, when we reached Las Vegas, I made the last-minute decision to have a drive-through wedding at one of those little wedding chapels to help her feel more secure about our relationship.

When I met Grace, I knew that she was in recovery for alcoholism. She was also newly recovered, but once someone goes through the 12 steps and puts God first in their life, they become a changed person. In hindsight, I realized that my experience with sobriety and someone else's are not necessarily the same thing. I had great hopes for her recovery and so did not truly recognize those red flags, and there were many, so many, during that road trip. Security truly comes from within a person. So, no matter what I did, I could not make her feel or act in any particular way or make her feel more secure.

By the time we returned to Florida, we had driven 18,000 miles, visiting 100 locations in 44 states. The entire trip took 55 days, but I cannot say it was peaches and cream. Despite the stressful circumstances, I had set the bar high with my first "Rugged Road Trip." Can you imagine the power of having 100 video testimonials about our dealers' successes with their businesses? What I had accomplished felt magnanimous, meeting our dealers spread throughout the states, greeting us with open arms and appreciation, and a renewed sense of confidence. This first trip certainly set the standard for any future road trips that would follow.

Chapter Nineteen

Looking from the window of the townhome I was renting, I felt as if I were on a stakeout. From here, I could watch the comings and goings of people to and from my house at all hours of the day and night. Grace, my soon-to-be ex-wife had been selling my things without my permission to finance her habits and had refused to leave when I asked her to. Until the situation could be resolved, my attorney had advised me to move out.

It was an uneasy feeling, not being in control of what was going on at my own doorstep. It felt like I was being held hostage. Being in this situation reminded me of something Jack had said to me years ago. "Darren. You're the only person I know that gets into relationships that end in litigation." What had transpired with the PMD lawsuit was now water under the bridge. In retrospect, being sued by Jack had actually turned out to be a blessing in the long run. Jack, however adversarial I thought he had been, had been right about my personal life in some ways. The first time we make a mistake we can call it a mistake. The second and subsequent times we make the same mistake, it is no longer a mistake, it is a decision, according to the famous author Paolo Coelho, with whom I wholeheartedly agree.

When Grace and I got married in Las Vegas less than a year ago, we had only known each other for six months, but that had never given me cause for concern. At the time, I felt as if we were meant to be together. In the beginning, our relationship was spontaneous and fun. But, as time passed, the red flags started flying. The problem was that I had not noticed them. Shortly into the relationship, she started showing some signs of paranoia. When my phone rang, she thought I was cheating on her. And after she had gotten to know my parents, she started calling them and accusing me of being unfaithful to her. I felt as if I had to continually defend myself. All of this drama made it hard for me to sleep at night. We had only been married for a short period of time when I realized that I could no longer be with a woman who did not trust me. We both agreed to end the relationship. She had never felt comfortable and secure, and she acted in ways that made me feel uncomfortable and insecure.

Happily, at the time, business was going well. Nearly a year had passed since last year's Rugged Road trip and this year's would be even bigger and better. I contacted several of our vendors, explaining that we wanted to give away some swag to the dealers. Kevin Mitchell, our national account rep, had tan-colored military-style survivalist backpacks made for the dealers. We also received tumblers, t-shirts, and hats with the "Rugged Road Trip 2020" logo printed on them. Bags, pens, travel packs, and measuring tapes were donated by other vendors as well. Because my soon-to-be ex-wife was selling everything that was being mailed to the house, I had everything sent to a friend's address instead. Even the wrapped Ford transit van that the company purchased for the trip was parked at another location.

To get the dealers pumped up about the upcoming trip, we had asked them to submit their ideas for the design of the van, which was going to be raffled to one lucky dealer after the road trip was done. The 2020 Rugged Road trip circular logo featured a curving roadway alongside mountains and trees. This logo took up most of the side of the van. The sliding door had a map of the continental U.S. with the words, "Empowering Rugged Entrepreneurs Coast to Coast" written across it.

Driving the van across the country also saved RSS money and time. The van would serve as my transportation, my accommodations, and my office during the trip. In the back of the van, we placed a mattress on a platform built by one of our contractors, and we also added a small desk in the back. With the van now packed to the brim with gifts for the dealers, there was no room for anything else. I had learned from the previous year that I did not need to pack a lot of clothes. I just packed some shirts, shorts, and flip flops, which was my normal wardrobe anyway. The trip now needed to be promoted. This was no problem for our savvy social media team who used the #ruggedroadtrip hashtag on all of the major social media sites, such as Facebook, Instagram, YouTube, and Twitter. I would also do my part by taking photos of the trip and doing live videos so our dealers could follow online.

Before I left on my trip, my divorce had been finalized. My attorney gave me the green light to move back into my home. I refortified my house, changed the locks, got security cameras, and buckled everything down. On the Fourth of July, I hit the gas pedal and embarked on RSS's second annual Rugged Road Trip. This year's route would be different than last year's. From my home in Jacksonville Beach, I travelled south on I-95 hugging the east coast of Florida, stopping at dealers along the way and passing through cities such as Daytona Beach, Melbourne, Port St. Lucie, and West Palm Beach. After reaching Miami, I travelled north to Fort Lauderdale taking Alligator Alley, an 80-mile stretch of I-75 that cuts through the Big Cypress Swamp and the Everglades, to the city of Naples on the west coast of the state. From there I continued on I-75 north, traversing the western coast of Florida then onto I-10 west through the panhandle to Louisiana and Texas.

In Texas we had more locations than we did in any other state. Visiting the dealers there would take some creativity. I called up Steve Silver, one of our vendors based in Dallas, and told him I was planning on hosting a barbeque nearby. Could he make it? It would be easier and more efficient to have some of the Texas dealers come to the barbeque rather than me driving to each store. Steve said he would not only come to the barbeque but that he would take me fishing the day before. I posted the event on Facebook, limiting the barbeque to 48 people, for a total of 50 including Steve and me, but I never expected more than a dozen people to show up. I was floored when our dealers from Texas, as well as other neighboring states, drove all the way to the barbeque to meet and eat with us. I had never realized the extent that people crave socializing. The need for them to feel they were a part of a community was necessary for them to thrive.

The barbeque over, my next stop was Waco, Texas, where I would be meeting with a dealer named Dustin Campbell. Dustin was a veteran, and I would describe him as a very serious man. He introduced me to his team, several men who were also veterans. Dustin had a stoic presence. He looked like a gladiator to me. He introduced me to his wife and his newborn baby. We chatted for a short while then took a photo together. Our visit was not long. Maybe 15 minutes or so. As

I was getting ready to leave, Dustin handed me an American flag. This was not any ordinary American flag. It was an 18-foot-long garrison flag, which I still have hanging in my garage today. He also gave me a box of smaller American flags to give to all of the dealers that I would be visiting. I was impressed and astounded by his generosity.

As I drove to my next destination, I reflected on my visit with Dustin, his wife, and his crew. He was a soldier. He had served our country and fought for our freedom. I felt honored to have met him and to receive the flag from him. However, I could not tell if my visit had made an impact. My goal in meeting with dealers is to build a rapport with them, so that they feel comfortable with me, and I with them. I pulled out my phone and gave Dustin's father-in-law, who was one of our coaches, a call. At BoxDrop®, we do not have managers. We have coaches. We like to say that we coach, guide, and mentor people rather than "manage" them.

Our coaches are dealers who have reached what we consider to be Level 3 in the business. Level 1 are those entrepreneurs who are just starting out. They run a 9-mattress store, and they sell their mattresses by appointment. Level 2 entrepreneurs offer more specialty items, such as specialty sleep mattresses, memory foam, and adjustable bases. Level 3 entrepreneurs are those who successfully run fully merchandised furniture stores, featuring living rooms, and bedrooms, etc. Dustin's father-in-law was such a person. When he picked up my call, I expressed how honored I felt to meet Dustin, and how much I enjoyed seeing his daughter and grandchild. The call was brief. It went well. And I thought nothing more of it.

I had been driving for a couple of hours when I received a text. I looked down at my phone. It was from Dustin. It was a long text message so I pulled over to the side of the road to read it. He wrote that he appreciated me stopping by. I was surprised but also happy that I had made such an impact on him. In fact, I could honestly say that he made more of an impact on me! Dustin wrote that he had done five tours in the six years that he was in the military, all overseas, and that he had been broken emotionally when he returned home. He said that his mattress business had changed his life, that it had given him a new start. Dustin's text message was a tear-jerking testimony. All of our dealers have a story to share, some more powerful than others. I realized that it is best not to assume anything about anybody because we never know what someone has gone through or is going through.

The next stop on my itinerary was Tyler, Texas, which may have seemed to some to be out of the way. That was true. I would be travelling in the opposite direction, but it was to see someone important to me. Not a dealer. But a girl. She and her husband had opened up a location 20 years ago, just when I was getting into this business. In fact, they were one of the first couples to open up a store. Sadly, her husband passed away at a young age, and she sold their furniture business. I had a soft spot for Sandy. She was a nice girl, very professional with a wonderful personality, and I was hoping we could work together again. I tried calling the old number I had for her in my phone. She still had the same number! When we first saw each other, we hugged, it had been such a long time, and I sensed a connection, a little electric spark. I spent the next two days visiting with her, hanging out, going kayaking. I also met her son, a pre-teen, who was a nice kid, very well-mannered. At the end of our brief visit, I headed west again. But I wasn't on the road for very long when my phone rang. I picked it up. It was Sandy.

"You know, Darren. This might sound weird, but for us to date, I have to have two things that are absolute," she said.

"Okay, Sandy."

"Well, you have to be debt-free, and you have to have your marriages in the Catholic Church annulled."

We chatted a bit then I ended the call. I was a bit surprised by her call. We had never discussed dating or any kind of romantic relationship when I visited. I also still had miles and miles to drive and many more dealers to meet.

On to New Mexico, then Arizona, California, and the Pacific Coast. From the east coast to the west, I had made 20 dealer visits by the time I reached Los Angeles. I would be picking up my best friend Valter at the L.A. airport so that we could have some buddy time, just like we used to when I was living in California. We visited Big Sur and Crater Lake and did some kayaking and hiking, and just had a great time. The plan was for us to drive up to Oregon, where Valter's sister had a store, but first, he accompanied me on a dealer visit, one that surprisingly showed me what the true spirit of entrepreneurship really meant.

We drove to Arroyo Grande where we met with Francine Black. Francine was happy and proud to tell us that she had just made $60,000 in profits the month before. But it had been a long, tough road to get to where she was today. She explained that when she first started out, she had no money, only a prayer. In fact, she had to borrow money to get started. That first year was a struggle to be sure. Money was tight, so she lived in her warehouse. But in her second year, she accomplished what we at BoxDrop® call a Rugged 300, which means she bought $300,000 in inventory. The difference was that she had spent her second year working with a coach, attending as many business training sessions as she could, and faithfully followed our business model. Throughout our conversation, she continually expressed how grateful she was for her business. It had truly changed her life. She even ended up getting remarried. Hers was truly a happily ever after story.

Feeling good about the visit with Francine, Valter and I then headed north to Oregon, to his sister's place, where he would remain and I would continue east to Montana. This was some of the most scenic driving I have ever done in America, and I was thankful for the iPad mounted to the windshield of the van which allowed me to make live videos as I drove through the national parks.

I had not forgotten about my conversation with Sandy. I had just put it on hold. Now that I had some free time I made a few phone calls and talked to a Catholic priest. I asked him about annulling my previous marriages and he asked me so many questions that I felt as if I were being interrogated. But that was okay. I needed to talk about my past. Needed to spill the emotions from my soul. I told him about my marriages to Melanie, to Chloe, and the latest one, to Grace.

"Were you married to any of these women in the Catholic church," he asked me.

"Well, no, Father," I replied. "I can't say that I was." I felt a little embarrassed, wondering where the course of this conversation was going.

"Well, then, if you were not married in the Catholic church, I cannot annul any of your marriages," he said.

"Oh, I see, Father."

"Because" he interjected, "they are not recognized as valid marriages. According to the Catholic Church, you have never been married. That's why I cannot annul these marriages."

Never been married. Amazing. It was as if those three marriages had been erased from my timeline. This could work, I thought. "Thank you, Father," I said as I hung up the phone.

I immediately called Sandy to tell her the news. "I have never been married according to the priest," I told her. "So, there are no marriages to annul."

"Then, come back and see me," she said.

It was a last-minute decision to head back to Tyler. The rerouting of my trip did allow me to see another 20 dealers along the way. Everyone at the company was aware that I had changed course, and everyone knew why. It was not a secret. When I arrived in Tyler, I got a hotel room and did not sleep at her house. We held hands and spent a lot of time talking. I stayed a few days before heading on the road again.

There were some common themes surrounding the dealer visits that I made. One of them was how BoxDrop® had fortuitously turned out to be a pandemic-proof business, because of our underlying business model of selling mattresses by appointment. Even if our dealers operated larger stores, they could still revert to the basic business model of advertising and selling by appointment only. We abided by our original model, and, because of it, our sales continued to grow. Sales have increased 50 percent. They might have been even higher if it were not for delays in the supply chain.

The manner in which we held our training sessions, however, had been somewhat affected, but not in a negative way. Our training sessions just became smaller and a little more personal. Our last traditional training was held in Houston in December 2019, with both new and experienced dealers. Our national conference in Louisville, Kentucky, in February 2020, was our last large conference. We cancelled our in-person training for the masses in March. Instead, I held Zoom trainings from my home office in Jacksonville Beach for those who wanted to attend remotely. Keeping with the regulations and guidelines of the state of Florida, we limited that training to 40 people, focusing on the new dealers. Instead of taking everyone out to dinner like I usually did, I had food catered and delivered to my house. For entertainment, we played games, such as ping pong and cornhole, and we spent time socializing. Everyone loved this new experience because it was authentic, neighborly, and fun, which is the best way to build a business and support people at the same time.

Two years prior, in 2018, RSS had also been blessed to acquire a franchise called bioPURE™, a disinfectant company which kills most bacteria and viruses, through spray technology that is broken down to miniscule levels and leaves no residue. The company had started in 2016, and RSS purchased it two years later. bioPURE™ franchises have spread throughout the country. During the second annual Rugged Road trip, I visited several bioPURE™ locations. On two occasions, I had the truck sprayed, once in New Orleans and another time in Johnson City, Tennessee, where bioPURE™ is headquartered. I also attended a bioPURE™ training after which I had planned on going to Ohio and Pennsylvania, then to New England before returning home to Florida. I cut my trip short, however, when the Ohio State football season was cancelled, which literally took the wind out of my sails because I am such a diehard fan. I skipped New England and headed home, having driven 14,000 miles in 49 days through 36 states, meeting with 108 dealers. Everywhere I went, the vendors were excited and thrilled about our visits. It meant a lot to them because it is a rarity these days to be visited by one of the owners of the company. This rings true to our company culture and mindset, which is that we are a giant family, and we are all interconnected.

When I returned to Jacksonville Beach, I flew Sandy and her son to Florida to visit me, thinking that her son would see my world, fall in love with it, and want to move there. My mindset was that this relationship with Sandy could possibly be a long-term one. Over the years she had gotten involved in MLM-style businesses, which she said felt exciting to her. She fell in love with the products and felt that they were the solution to everything. She was also active in the marketing of the products. It seemed as if every time we went to the beach, however, she would ask me to take pictures and videos of her for her platform. Everything became a commercial to her and, after a short while, that became exhausting. Her son enjoyed the trip to Florida but he did not want to leave Texas. He had friends there and he had school. Would I relocate to Tyler, she asked? The thought of moving was tempting at first. I would be in a relationship with someone I cared about and maybe eventually have a family. But my heart was in Florida. My house was there, my dad was there, my business was based there. It was then that I realized that I might be repeating the same pattern that I usually did in most of my personal relationships. I was about to base my actions on emotional decisions rather than thinking things through. For the time being, I decided to hold off on any kind of long-term involvement with Sandy and remain where my life was stable, right here, in Florida.

Chapter Twenty

Barbeque, burgers and burritos. In that order. If I could describe RSS's third annual Rugged Road Trip, the delicious regional foods that I enjoyed with the dealers I visited was a big part of the experience. Sharing meals and creating a fellowship with dealers was the most important part of the trip. I did not feel that it was the time to be concerned about eating mindfully. I could focus on that once I returned to Florida. My goal was not to change the way our dealers do business, but rather, it was to know them better and to build relationships with them. Our dealers are interesting people of all ages, from single persons, to families, to retired couples, from all walks of life and from all parts of the country. My mission was to form connections with all of them.

In late June 2021, I was ready to embark on yet another cross-country road trip. By now, BoxDrop® had 470 stores throughout the country. In the past six years, I had visited nearly 300 locations, during past Rugged Road trips and/ or See America trainings. This year, however, my itinerary would be less ambitious than it had been in previous years. These trips required physical and mental energy, and I often returned feeling exhausted and drained. The trip was work, but always fun work.

This year I decided to visit half of the number of dealers that I usually did, as well as the number days I would be driving. My goal was to meet 50 dealers in 20 days. I wanted to make quality visits with new dealers and with those dealers whom I had not previously met.

Before leaving, I decorated the inside of the van with stickers of all shapes and sizes creating a collage of various U.S. destinations and hung the traditional Route 66 metal road sign that was signed by dealers on the first Rugged Road trip. The van was wrapped with a colorful artist's rendition of a United States geographical map, with vibrant blues, greens, and yellows. Our RSS, BoxDrop® and Rugged Road trip logos, along with the tagline, "400 locations nationwide and growing," were also painted on the exterior of the van. Just as we did last year, we intended to raffle off the van to the dealers after the trip.

The back of the transit van was loaded with gifts for the dealers, such as hand-held American flags, Rugged Road trip photo frames, hats, travel pillows, travel cups, and Sleep2Win khaki backpacks. This year the t-shirts had been sponsored by the Steve Silver Company in Forney, Texas.

I placed our mascot, a cute stuffed sloth, in the passenger's seat beside me and took off. My route was a northward one, through Georgia, North Carolina, and Virginia, before stopping in Johnson City, Tennessee, where I attended an RSS board meeting. Afterwards, I stayed at Scott and Daphene's lake house on Lake Watauga in the Cherokee National Forest for a couple of days. What beautiful country! The lake is clean and cool and surrounded by 360° mountain views and is actually a reservoir that resulted when a dam was constructed in the 1940's to revive the area. Not many people are aware that the original town of Butler, Tennessee, was buried beneath that lake, and that there is a new town of Butler that now borders it.

During my visit to Tennessee, I saw firsthand how Scott has helped revive Johnson City. He has partnered with Scott Callahan, owner of Tennessee Hills Distillery in Jonesborough, Tennessee, to build a whiskey distillation plant, museum, and restaurant, and future hotel. That partnership has also worked with East Tennessee State University to create a distillation and fermentation sciences minor at the school. Today, and throughout the years, Scott has shown his heart of gold by his sincerity in wanting to help others.

I continued driving through our country's heartland, so onward through West Virginia, Kentucky, Indiana, and Missouri I went. On the Fourth Of July, I visited with a dealer couple and stopped at an antique store in Lake Girardeau, Missouri, where I purchased a cotton, hand-sewn 4' x 6' American flag to hang inside of the van, keeping the road trip in sync with the same patriotic tradition many of our dealers followed in their own places of business. Late in the afternoon, I was invited to attend an Independence Day concert, complete with speeches by city officials followed by a medley of patriotic songs played by the local orchestra. As I drove throughout our nation's heartland, the theme was consistently "I love America."

Continuing through Missouri, my plan was to meet with three generations of BoxDrop® owners, all of whom owned locations. I met with Chris Herion, who owned a location in Independence, Kansas, the name of the city which I thought was fitting for this particular trip, on July 6. The day before

I met her grandson, Justin Herion, who owned a location in Lake of the Ozarks, Missouri, then her son, Randy Herion, in Bolivar, Missouri afterwards. When I first arrived at Chris's store, I observed her helping a customer and offered to help her load the customer's truck at the warehouse. Chris was of the Apostolic faith, and I highly admired that. "I love your community," I said to her without intention.

"That's because you love God and we are connected," she answered naturally. When you have God in your life, you feel a connection with others who also have God in their lives." I thought about her answer, and I believed it to be true.

On July 8, my trip took an additional turn for the better. I was on my way to Kansas City, Missouri, to visit Brad Loy, a member of RSS's leadership team and a good friend. As I pulled into his driveway, he was waiting for me in his front yard with his new wife, Amy. I barely had time to roll down my window, when he pointed out that the time of my arrival was 11:22 a.m. Brad knew full well the significance of 11-22 to me. Not only was November 22 the date I had decided to become sober, 11:22 also held spiritual significance for me, specifically, that no matter what, God is always looking out for me.

In the King James version (KJV) of the Bible, the Gospel of Mark 11:22 reads, "[21] And Peter calling to remembrance saith unto him, Master, behold, the fig tree which thou cursedst is withered away. *[22]* **And Jesus answering saith unto them, Have faith in God".** In addition, the Gospel of John 11:21-22 reads, "[21]Then said Martha unto Jesus, Lord, if thou hadst been here, my brother [Lazarus] had not died. *[22]* **But I know that even now, whatsoever thou wilt ask of God, God will give it thee."**

Back in 2007, when I had moved to Jacksonville Beach, I was occasionally attending services at the Beach United Methodist Church, but I never joined. The church had a worship team called Eleven22. After I became sober, a church was started called, "The Church of Eleven22™." It offered a contemporary church service at 11:22. Everywhere I went in the city, I saw the church's promotional stickers. The continual reminder of the date 11-22 kept me focused on my sobriety. I hung onto my sobriety date. I hung onto having faith in God. I had God in my life and He wanted me to think about Him and my sobriety. That is what helped me focus. It showed me that God was always putting steps in front of me. I just had to take them.

I looked at my watch. Brad was correct. *It was 11:22 a.m.* I did not realize it at the time, but a new spiritual journey was about to be set in motion, one which would catapult me into another level of my relationship with God.

It was also a great joy to be spending time with Brad and Amy. Their marriage was like gold. It was attractive and magical, the type of relationship that I craved for myself. They had met at church where they were both prayer leaders. It was obvious that they had made a commitment to one another and to God. They had dated with purpose and waited to be intimate until they were married. When Brad had first confided this to me, it seemed strange. But, as time went on, I could see the importance of it.

My plan for the evening was to do laundry at their place, then take them out to dinner before leaving early the next day. Sometimes, however, our plans do not turn out the way we intend them to. When I mentioned going out to dinner, Brad and Amy said that they already had plans for the evening. They were going to attend an event that evening at the

Forerunner Church in Kansas City, a nondenominational church with contemporary worship. Would I like to come? Of course, I would. Before we headed out, Brad made us dinner. All the while I kept an open mind. *God, what do you want me to hear*?

That night six separate ministries gathered at the Forerunner Church for worship and prayer. The International House of Prayer, established by Mick Bickle, had established nonstop 24/7 prayer rooms throughout the world; Eric Metaxas, a Yale graduate and public speaker, and radio host and a prolific writer, who signed a copy of his book entitled, *Bonhoeffer: Pastor, Martyr, Prophet, Spy*, a biography of a German Lutheran pastor against the Nazi occupation during WWII; Andy Byrd of Youth with A Mission (YWAM); Frances Chan from Peace and Love Ministries; Chris Reed, an apostolic healer, of Chris Reed Ministries; and, Ken Fish, from Orbis Ministries, Inc.™ I also was able to meet John G. Elliot, a songwriter and worship leader, who had made a video on revelation.

When we arrived at the church, the seats were filled, and it stayed so the entire night. People sang on stage and gave their testimonies. People were being healed. I could feel the power of God within the walls of the church. It was an intense evening, an emotional experience for me, and, on several occasions, I was brought to tears. At the end of the event, the people filed out of the church and the lights were turned off. The sky had grown dark, but the parking lot was alive with people chatting outside. I thanked Brad and Amy for inviting me to their church. I felt rejuvenated, but I was ready to go to bed, get up early, and get back on the road.

"Are you coming tomorrow night?" Amy asked.

"Well, I am supposed to be on a road trip," I said. "Let me

think about it. I'll pray about it," I added. The next day came and I found myself still at the Loy's house getting ready to go to church again. Staying one more day in Kansas City would not negatively impact the road trip. That night, the second night, was even more spiritually powerful than the first, and that is what made all the difference.

The three of us returned to the house that evening. Brad turned to me and said, "Darren, the Lord is telling me to give you this."

"What is it, Brad?"

He handed me a Bible. His personal Bible. "So, are you coming again tomorrow?"

"Of course, I am." My response was automatic. Of course, I was staying another day.

After the third night, I did not want to leave the church. All I wanted was to do was be with the masses of people who were worshipping the Lord and experience the energy surrounding us. The next day, the fourth day, was going to be a Sunday morning service. I had already planned to go. No one had to invite me. I was drawn to the church, to the entire experience. All around me were people who loved God, people with whom I could talk to about God and about my faith.

After the Sunday service, I got back on the road feeling more comfortable about my faith. I had always believed in God, I had always had faith that things were going to work out, but what I had experienced for the past three days was spiritually powerful. It had changed me. As I drove through Missouri, Nebraska, South Dakota, then Colorado, I felt different. In Colorado, I stopped in the city of Fort Collins, where I met with a dealer named Lori. Lori was a petite woman who was as tough as nails. We had lunch together and I shared with her my experiences in Kansas City with the Loys. She told me that a similar event had just happened in her community as well. To me, it felt as if God was saying, "Look, I'm doing this world-wide, across the country, not just in Kansas City."

After stops in Denver, Castle Rock, and Pueblo, I headed north to St. George, Utah, then Lake Havasu City, Arizona, near the California border, before meeting with David and Darla Staten in Cottonwood, Arizona. I had met the couple in Jacksonville Beach at a training session several months before, in January 2021. After that training session in January, Darla asked if I would like to have coffee. We all agreed to meet at the coffee shop across the street from my house where Darla started teaching me about the Bible. "You need to be baptized," she said to me directly. "Okay," I answered. That was that. We walked across the street to my house where she baptized me in my backyard swimming pool. Here was an older, mature woman, wearing a long dress standing in my swimming pool giving me a single dunk under the water! *That was the fourth time I have been baptized, and I do not think a person can be over-baptized.*

That day I felt better. I was no longer uncomfortable in honoring the relationship I had with Jesus, my Lord and Savior. Since then, I have been talking to Him every day and building my relationship with Him. As a result, there has been change in my life and the blessings I have received have been unbelievable!

After visiting with David and Darla in Arizona, I turned around and headed toward home, stopping in Roswell, New Mexico, ironically my 51st stop. Then, on through Texas. I stopped in Denton, which is north of Dallas, where I met with James White. During our conversation, he mentioned that his dad had been a worship leader for YWAM for 20 years. That to me seemed like another confirmation of the synchronicity of God's connection. So was the visit with the rodeo pastor I had met in College Station, Texas, Todd Keller. I had breakfast with Todd and his wife Darla. As we were getting ready to leave the restaurant, he asked me with appreciation in his eyes what hat size I wear. Being a Floridian who does not usually wear a cowboy hat, I had no idea. Todd took the hat off of his head and put it on mine. Oftentimes, the dealers will give me little gifts along the way. But, when a pastor or preacher gives you a gift, is it like God is offering you a gift.

As I reached Louisiana and Alabama, visiting dealers along the way and wearing my new cowboy hat, I was eager to get back home. My last stop was to pay George and Sandi Varn a quick visit at their beach house on Florida's forgotten coast. After vising 71 dealers in 22 states in 35 days, I would soon be home.

Before heading into my house, I decided to check my mailbox for some reason. Inside was a heavy, rectangular package from the David and Darla Staten in Arizona. Inside was a hardcover King James Bible with my name, Darren B. Conrad, embossed in gold upon the cover. On the inside cover, Darla had written in cursive, "Darren, we are so proud of you." The Bible was such a thoughtful gift and also a spiritually profitable one. As I reflected upon my trip, I realized that for me this second annual Rugged Road Trip had been about more than just dealer visits. I had made long-lasting spiritual connections, experienced the patriotism that still exists in our country today, and felt God's hand upon our nation.

Chapter Twenty-One

After I returned from the road trip, I spent a lot of time reflecting on my visit to the Forerunner Church in Kansas City. One of Frances Chan's sermons had especially spoken to me. That sermon was about leadership in the church. Frances Chan said that leadership was not about feeding one's ego. Instead, leadership was about helping, guiding, and motivating the younger generation so that they could and would want to lead. I thought about my own leadership role at RSS. Currently, I was the only person in the company who was serving as national trainer. Chan's words inspired me to rethink that role and to consider letting go, even though my ego still longed to be known as the "expert".

Leaving my role as national trainer for RSS would certainly be an act of surrendering, which has been a recurrent theme throughout my life. In 2008, I had surrendered to alcohol once I realized that my life had become unmanageable due to my drinking. In 2015, I had surrendered the company I had built from scratch which had, in my opinion, been taken away from me. And, then again, in 2017, when I began working for RSS in an official capacity, I also surrendered to being the guy in charge, the head honcho, the CEO, and instead became a part of the company's dynamic leadership team.

Before I embarked on the third Rugged Road trip, the RSS team had already been tossing the idea around of putting Josh Haines into a leadership position within the company. If I were to step down as national trainer, Josh, then, would logically be my replacement. He was sharp, witty, intelligent, and, more importantly, he was running a successful location. I had not owned a store in such a long time that I could no longer teach by example. By stepping aside and asking Josh to lead, the next generation could then take over, which would ultimately contribute to the longevity of the company.

I could still continue my role as the "guy who drives around the country visiting dealers." In the future, those annual Rugged Road trips might take a different form, although I had no idea at the present what that form could possibly be. One option was to visit more dealers over a longer period of time. Another might be making visits to fewer dealers in a series of smaller trips throughout the year.

I had also been considering starting another franchise under the RSS umbrella. Still an entrepreneur at heart, I could also work as a consultant, helping other companies succeed with my training system that had worked so well in the mattress industry. Starting a new company was another option. These were all great ideas. But what I knew for sure was that I did not have to make any plans. Most importantly, I needed to be open to wherever God would lead me next.

Only one thing was certain. If I had learned anything in my 51 years, it was to stop making plans. God's plans have always been so different than my plans, and His plans were the right plans. My plans, no matter how good they seemed to me at the time, never came to fruition. At this point in my life, I could no longer say, "Here's the next chapter. Here's the direction I am going." Instead, I chose to move forward with faith without knowing exactly what God had in store for me. I just knew that I had to trust that if I stayed in alignment with Him, everything would keep getting better. And it did. Whenever I decided to surrender my own plans, including what I thought I needed to do and what I thought was good for me, I was able to accept God's plan for me, which was always more of a blessing than I could ever have imagined.

There was one area of my life, however, where I had not yet surrendered. I had always wanted to have a meaningful personal relationship. That is not to say I did not seek love or a good relationship. I have. Over the years, I had been trying too hard to find that perfect someone to share my life with. When I did meet someone, I would try to mold them into whom I wanted them to be, instead of trusting God to pick the right person for me. Before I had embarked upon this year's road trip, I had been dating a woman whose company I enjoyed. But there was something that did not feel right about our relationship. After spending time with Brad and Amy and seeing how beautiful and Godly their marriage was, I craved the same kind of relationship for myself. It's not that the woman I was dating was not a nice or a good person. It was just that I could not check off the "spiritual" boxes because our relationship was more physical than spiritual. On the road trip, my idea of what I wanted in a relationship had changed. I wanted a relationship where both of us had mutual trust in and love for the Lord! Once I returned to Jacksonville, I planned on sharing my thoughts and feelings with her in person, but I still had many more dealers to visit and miles to drive before we could have that conversation.

On these road trips, I was very blessed to meet with so many wonderful people, but there were also hours upon hours where I would be driving through flatlands, deserts, or mountains, sometimes not seeing a car for miles. On one of those driving days, I felt compelled to pray aloud. I called out, "God, I give up. I am done. If you have someone for me, then please bring them to me at the right time. I am not going to pick anymore." I spoke like this for at least an hour. Once I was done exhausting my words and my prayers, I knew that all I had to do was wait. This was about God's timing and not my timing.

I stopped the car to post some photos and videos of the trip to our Rugged Road Trip social media sites and noticed that I had received a friend request from a woman. It was unusual for me to receive a request from someone I did not know. I accepted it and thought no more about it. The next day, I received a message from her that said, "I like your picture. You look like a fun guy." Now, I was still on the road and had several more weeks of travelling. I also felt uneasy about responding because I was still officially in a relationship, so I ignored the message.

Once I got home, I spent a few days unpacking the truck, getting some rest, and easing back into my life. I arranged to meet the woman I was currently seeing. After our meeting, we both agreed to end the relationship and we parted ways amicably with no hard feelings.

By now, I had forgotten about the woman who had messaged me until she wrote again. "I'm surprised that we have not met before, seeing that we have a lot of friends in common."

I thought about responding, then quickly wrote, "We should meet for coffee."

She responded that she was currently out of town. I wrote that I had a trip to Las Vegas for work. So, we both agreed to get together after I returned. While she was away, I scrolled through her profile but did not feel as if she would be the kind of person I would be interested in. She was very pretty and looked nice. I just could not put my finger on why I felt this way. It was just a hunch. One month went by and we were both finally back in town. She contacted me and we agreed to meet for coffee. There would be no harm in just meeting for coffee.

The conversation went well, and she invited me to attend her church the next day, which interested me. She said she was part of the worship team, so I sat in the congregation while she was on stage singing. I liked the energy of the church. I liked the feel of it. The people were friendly, and the worship music was heartfelt and meaningful. After the service, I asked her if she wanted to go out to dinner with me the next day and she said yes.

I took her to St. Augustine, America's oldest city, for dinner at a restaurant that overlooked the Matanzas River. Ponce de Leon, a Spanish explorer, was said to have landed there while looking for the Fountain of Youth on Bimini in the Bahamas, even though the exact location of de Leon's landing has later been said to be further south on the Atlantic coast. The city of St. Augustine, which has changed hands under Spanish, French, and English leadership, is known for its coquina rock fort, Castillo de San Marcos, now a national monument.

Besides being an historical city, St. Augustine is also a romantic city, and a perfect place for a first date. The phenomenal architecture, large oak trees and grass-lined squares, and cobblestone roads with horse and carriage, and the oldest construction in America, predating even the original thirteen colonies. We strolled hand-in-hand down St. George Street, the main pedestrian thoroughfare with its quaint shops, boutiques, and coffee shops. As we were walking down the street, something compelled me to stop and look into her eyes. I turned to her and said, "I'm not looking for a casual, physical relationship. I am looking for a Godly relationship with the right woman." As the words tumbled out of my mouth, I could not believe I had said them. I had been thinking these thoughts for a while but this was not usually something I would say on a first date. Allie was amazed at what I said and expressed that no one had ever said anything to her like this before. At that moment, I realized how much I had changed. God was now first and foremost in my life.

During my Kansas City visit, when I had been attending the Forerunner Church, one of the themes that was continually being discussed was family and how the ultimate selfless act was the raising of children. I did not have any children. I did not have an heir. I had no one to leave a legacy. Still, I had a heartfelt desire to have a family. I needed children in my life. Some members of the church told me that there were so many children who did not have parents. I considered adopting a child. Throughout the road trip, I had met with dealers who had adopted children and said their lives had been changed for the better.

Allie had three children under the age of 12, God had not only put her into my life, He had also blessed me with the possibility of becoming a stepfather. *At this time in my life, I now felt up to the challenge of being a dad.* God was moving my heart in ways I had never thought could have been possible before.

That summer, I got to know Allie better. I realized that in some ways our lives were parallel. We both had experienced similar obstacles during our childhood. We both had attended college around the same time, even though she was several years younger than me. We both loved exercising and we both enjoyed the outdoors.

Most importantly, we both loved God. We both loved our country. Could she possibly be the woman with whom I should start a new life? Meeting her and her children seemed like it could lead to a happy ending. There was only one way to find out.

In September, I invited her to attend RSS's incentive trip in Mexico with me. Yes, it would be a company trip and, yes, we would be going with 600 other people, including RSS leadership, vendors, and dealers, so it would be a little crowded. But the resort was a big place, so I felt we would be able to carve out a little personal time to do some things together, just the two of us.

I had been carrying a ring in my pocket, but I did not have a plan for how and when I would propose to her. I felt that I would just know when the time was right to pop the question. On the third night of the trip, when the company activities were drawing to a close, I took her for a walk on the beach. We spent hours talking, walking, and watching the waves. When the moment felt right, I placed the ring upon her finger and spoke what was in my heart. "Are you proposing to me," she asked. I smiled and she said, "yes." The proposal was not grand or fancy. It just felt natural and the way that a proposal should happen.

The ring, too large, slipped from her finger, even though it was the right size. "I'll get it resized as soon as we get back home, honey," I told her as I hugged her, thinking nothing of it. When we returned to Florida, one of the first things I did was get the ring resized, but it was still too big. In fact, I had the ring resized four times and each time it was still too big. Because the ring kept slipping off of her finger, she did not wear it.

I had made a vow to the Lord that I would remain chaste until I was married. When I first told her about it, on our first date in St. Augustine, we both agreed to this plan. But then, somewhere along the way, she changed her mind. To make her happy, I broke that vow, but then I immediately regretted my decision. I had made her happy, but I was no longer happy.

In my prayers, I cried out to God and said, "If doors need to be shut, then please shut them, Lord."

Ever since we returned from Mexico, Allie and I had a nightly routine. After her kids were tucked into bed, she would call me on the phone at 8:30 p.m. sharp. One night, however, she did not call. The next day there was a knock upon my door. It was Allie with a small box in her hand. She asked me if I wanted to go back to dating to see where it might lead. I thought about her suggestion but felt it was now too late. I did not want the relationship to move backwards.

It was a humbling experience, having an engagement ring returned to me. I also felt a bit embarrassed. Everyone in my company knew that I was engaged. But I think I felt more embarrassed for myself. I had not seen the red flags. I just wanted that magical fairytale ending and had jumped into proposing to Allie without thinking things through. Everything had seemed so perfect. Like the plan was unfurling itself before me. Obviously, I had been mistaken.

I have always believed that people have come into my life for a reason, if only to teach me something about myself. What did meeting Allie teach me? Obviously that I should take my time and get to know someone before rushing into a relationship and letting things get too serious too quickly. That was a pattern that needed to be broken.

But there was also something else that meeting Allie prompted me to do. I knew that in order to truly be ready for a relationship that I would have to break my previous soul ties. After we got engaged, I cleaned out my house and got rid of photos, knick knacks, and mementos that reminded me of previous relationships. I ripped out my carpets and painted all of the rooms in my home. I spent a lot of time preparing a foundation for a future lasting love. But this would not be for love of a woman. This would be for a love of God.

I had made a vow to the Lord that I would be faithful and I would keep that vow, even if I had to walk that path alone, always remaining faithful that the Lord would provide.

I returned to the jewelers with the ring. I was hoping to get a refund but I was not expecting it. I sat for a moment in the parking lot and pulled out the box with the ring and prayed aloud. "If this is Your will and Your way, Lord, then let this be an easy process and return this ring and be done." I got out of the car, walked into the jewelers, and got a full refund with no questions asked.

That Thanksgiving I drove to Ohio to spend the holiday with my parents, all the way listening to a CD called *Learn the Bible in 24 Hours.* My plan was to listen to the first half on the way there and then the second half on the way back. I used to have objections and reservations about some of what I read in the Bible. But, on that trip, all of my questions had been answered. I learned more about the Bible driving to and from Ohio than I ever had during my entire lifetime, which

I probably would not have been prompted to do had I not gone down this path. It was like God was saying to me, "Drive and while you are driving, you are going to learn." This just confirmed and reaffirmed my faith and convictions that Jesus Christ is our Messiah. I never thought I would say that aloud before. I never felt comfortable vocalizing my beliefs. Just like I thought I would never go to recovery meetings and become sober when I was younger. In fact, my life turned out to be the total opposite of what I thought it would be.

On my way back to Florida, a dealer in South Carolina called me. It happened to be a pocket dial call, but what I have learned throughout my life is that nothing happens by accident. The dealer and I talked for a short while and he invited me to go to his church, Morning Star Ministries, a prophetic ministry started by Rick Joyner in Fort Mill, where Chris Reed was now a prophetic minister. I had actually been listening to Chris Reed since my visit to Kansas City and wanted to go to his church in person so I accepted the invitation.

When I arrived, three people who called themselves prophets greeted me and invited me into the church. Two of them said I was about to get busy with work and they all agreed that I was going through a transition period. "You have a beautiful heart. This warm, caring heart, and He sees it," said one of the prophets. She told me that all of my trials and tribulations were over and that God was pouring oil over me to heal me. The last prophet said that he saw a calm lake with trees changing colors. He said he saw me in a peaceful, calm place. On the drive home to Florida, I felt renewed in spirit. I was also looking forward to the upcoming year, 2022. The RSS national conference would be held in mid-January at the Gaylord in Dallas, and I felt it was going to be monumental.

Heading home, I did not know what 2022 would bring, but

there was one thing I knew for sure. Throughout my life, God has always been my director. More recently, I am more than comfortable saying that Jesus Christ is my director, too. I look to the Holy Trinity: God the Father, Jesus, who is God the Son, and God, the Holy Spirit. I am not professing to be a saint. I am not perfect. All I can say is that I crave God because His presence has touched my life.

Chapter Twenty-Two

More than five years ago, on July 26, 2016, I met with a man at Buddy Todd Park in Oceanside, California, a man who has since become a good friend, spiritual guide, and mentor. When I first made David's acquaintance, he was in his mid-seventies, around the age of my parents. I would describe him as creative, in good shape, and an author and avid hiker. He was a lover of nature who worked in, lived in, and was passionate about our nation's forests. When we met that day, we talked about the future, specifically the next five years of my future. He introduced to me a concept called "surrendering" which he learned about from a book that became like a lifeline for me, *The Surrender Experiment: My Journey into Life's Perfection* by Michael A. Singer. At the time, I was not familiar with surrender training. I was always putting one foot forward, never really knowing exactly what the future would bring, but having a plan for how I would like it to work out. Yes, in the past, I had set big plans in motion. Very big plans. However, these plans rarely, if any, came to fruition. Something bigger and always better happened instead.

As I sat with David on that park bench, taking in the sights and sounds of nature, and talking about the future, he asked me what I would like my life to be like in the next five years. That was difficult for me to foresee. At the time, I was living in California with only a few belongings and articles of clothing to my name. There was a 60-day jail sentence awaiting me if I dared return to Florida. I also had to abide by a temporary injunction due to lawsuits filed against me personally and against my company, disallowing me from starting any new business in the mattress industry in which I now enjoyed working. I had spent years developing and was continuing to develop a successful and full-proof system for running businesses, specifically in the mattress industry, that I had given away to a competitor, Scott Andrew, who also became a friend, with hopes that it would help not only the dealers I had worked with over the years, but also the new ones that started businesses under the RSS umbrella. That gift was given upon a premise of hope and a belief that Scott would follow through on his promises that I would receive part-ownership of RSS in the future. For two years, I was not an official employee of RSS, yet I had spent my time travelling around the country building a company that I was not yet officially a part of.

I was just living on hope and faith that everything would turn out for the best, although I was not sure how that would happen.

David started asking me questions and I answered to the best of my ability. We discussed things that most people talk about, such as family, finances, health and personal goals, as well as places where I would like to work and live. I knew that I wanted and needed more stability in my life. I had already become and was maintaining my sobriety, attending recovery meetings and making life-long friends along the way, since 2008, which had been a monumental step for me. I was not doing as well as I would have liked in the personal relationship department, often meeting nice and not-so-nice women, but none were ones that I believed could truly be a lifelong partner. My finances had also taken a hit due to the many lawsuits filed against me and my companies over the years as well. With all of these current happenings, it would be difficult for anyone to believe that my life could turn around in five years, but I believed it would.

I was very happy and thankful for what I did have. I think that is one important point to consider. No matter what is happening in our lives, good or bad or in between, we should always be grateful for what we do have. When God's plans unfolded before me, regardless of if I had fallen or had made a mistake, I recognized them as divine intervention. His plans were so much better than mine, so I decided to go with the flow and follow His lead instead.

Now in regard to my five-year plan, my main goals were to return to Florida, specifically to the beach, to be welcomed as part of the RSS team with part-ownership, to meet the woman of my dreams and raise a family, to be financially fit and debt-free, and to maintain my physical fitness, health, and well-being. Those were my main goals, among other smaller, personal goals.

Shortly after meeting with David, I received a one-year anniversary card from Scott in the mail with a check for a small amount. His gesture was proof to me that he would keep his word.

In 2017, Scott's promise was manifested when I officially joined the RSS team as CMO and became part-owner of the company. For the first time in my life, I was in a superior financial position. My debt had been cleared due to my previous business partner buying out Mattress Direct in bankruptcy court, and from my working with an accountant to pay my IRS debt in full. With the lawsuit settled and the jail sentence dropped, I was also free to return to Florida. I am a beach person, so I moved back to Jacksonville Beach and rented a bright and airy condo with an ocean view. At RSS, I continued my role as national trainer and started undertaking cross-country road trips, the Rugged Road Trips, meeting multitudes of dealers, both new and successful, throughout the country. That turnaround in my life would be enough for anyone's faith to grow in leaps and bounds, and I can say that mine did grow. But it was not until the 2021 Rugged Road Trip that I had a spiritual awakening and became closer to God, the Holy Trinity, more than I ever had been in my life.

After the 2021 Rugged Road trip, I also realized the magnanimous impact that my visits with the dealers had made. Jerry Williams forwarded me a letter that had been sent to the corporate offices in Dublin, Ohio, while I was away on the trip. The letter was from one of the dealers I visited. She wrote how valued she and her family felt by being visited by a member of the company's executive team, and especially that I would make such an effort to visit her store and meet with her in person. I knew that I would need to continue following that company tradition no matter what form it might take in the future.

As the end of my five-year plan was approaching, I had achieved nearly everything on my list. I had become more financially fit and viable, moved back to the beach, was healthy and in good shape, etc. However, there were two things which I had not yet achieved: Obtaining my real estate license (which was not as important to me) and starting and raising a family (which was extremely important to me).

I did not think anything of it until I started scrolling through some of my past messages. My spine shivered when I realized that Allie had messaged me on July 26, 2021, at 5:54 p.m., exactly five years to the day I had executed my first five-year plan with David. *Better late than never, I smiled to myself.* Even though that relationship did not work out as I had wanted it to, I knew that God had other plans for me. Meeting Allie had sent me on a different trajectory than I would have undertaken. I was now preparing myself to be in a Godly relationship, so that when I did meet the right person, I would be ready. In looking back, I realized that my life has always been a series of trajectories, none of which I would not have taken on my own, but only through my faith in God was I able to travel down a different path than I once envisioned.

At the end of August 2021, I flew back to California to meet and interview again with my friend, guide, and mentor David, about my next five-year-plan, which I am hopeful about more now than ever. It had been a while since we had seen each other, and it felt like I was home again, my temporary California home on the west coast when I had been stranded from the east. Seeing him was an emotional experience. It takes a lot to surrender at first, to be humble and follow God's lead with faith and thankfulness. I had already surrendered to alcohol, so I knew what surrendering felt like, but my biggest surrender was letting go of the legal battles and becoming part of a team. When I surrendered and let the Lord be first and foremost in my life, that is when my success in business changed for the better.

To mark the end of 2021 with a happy occasion, my little brother got married to the love of his life on December 31st. Though he is younger than me, he has taught me a lot about love and about relationships, through his example. The wonderful woman that he married, he had been seeing for six years before they took their vows. All of my family up north are members of the Roman Catholic Church, so it was important to my brother and his bride to have a spiritual wedding. Their wedding ceremony was beautiful, and authentic, and I felt moved being his best man and a part of that very special day.

Will I be next in line to take my vows? That is only for God to tell. It has not been revealed to me as of yet. And I am okay with that. All I know is that when she does come into my life that I will be ready to surrender once again, but it will be a surrendering that I am most looking forward to: Becoming part of a family to raise and grow all of us in the Lord. This will be my biggest blessing of all. When it happens, I will be thankful for it. I know that everything I ask for in prayer with faith will allow God's plans to continue to unfold before me. I just have to have faith and believe before I ask and receive and be willing to follow Him.

Epilogue

Perhaps some people may have never heard of the city of Grapevine, Texas, but it served as a magnificent location for RSS's National Conference in mid-January of 2022, specifically at the Gaylord Texan Resort and Convention Center, just northwest of Dallas on the shores of Lake Grapevine.

Our more than 800 attendees, including dealers, vendors, and RSS employees, enjoyed the Texan theme of the conference as well as the opportunity to don cowboy hats, boots, and traditional western garb to get into the spirit of the event. The resort's 40,000-square-foot showroom was an excellent place for the trade show. It also had spacious rooms for break-out sessions for those who wanted to participate in classes. Some of our special sessions were specifically for our veterans to honor them for their service to our country.

One of the highlights of this year's convention was our motivational speaker, Inky Johnson. During his football college career, Inky sustained an injury while playing for the University of Tennessee. He gave an inspirational message of hope and faith and how to keep going when things get tough.

Another highlight was our vendor partner, Nectar Mattresses, one of the top mattress companies in the world.

One of my roles was to give away our Rugged Road Trip van to one lucky dealer at the end of the conference. That was not such an easy thing to do. I had grown a bit attached to the van, since it had been my faithful companion on the 2020 and 2021 Rugged Road Trips. Heading to the conference, I drove the van from Jacksonville to Grapevine, stopping to visit dealers on Florida's panhandle, Louisiana, and Texas. Before raffling her off, I had her washed and detailed for that one lucky dealer who would be driving her away. Ten finalists would be selected throughout the course of the three-day conference.

At last year's conference, we also attempted to give away a van. Let's just say that the winner did not think they could use the van, so I was blessed to drive her for another year. This year, however, we were going to do things a bit differently. The dealers would need to be qualified. First of all, they needed to be a member of the Big 300 Club, meaning they had ordered at least $300,000 of product within the past year. Secondly, they could not be employed by RSS and, thirdly, they had to be present to win.

Before and during the conference, I spent time building the momentum for the drawing which would take place on the last night in the grand ballroom.

That evening finally came and I found myself on the stage, emceeing the event, with ten finalists on stage all wanting to draw the winning ticket. The suspense did not last long, however, as Rick Coney, the second person to draw an envelope, won the van. He and his wife were excited and grateful. They drove the van all the way back to Salt Lake City.

For this year's coming cross-country trip, the company has already purchased a new van and, in the summer, I'll be heading out on the road once again. I have received so many blessings from the Lord, including going on these trips every year to inspire our dealers and to be inspired by them. I have nowhere to look now but to the future, fully knowing in the present, with the Lord in the driver's seat, that I am and will always be a part of THE RUGGED ROAD TRIP!

For readers who would like to keep in touch and find out more about The Rugged Road Trip, please visit https://darren-brettconrad.com or follow @RuggedRoadTrip on Facebook, Twitter, and Instagram.

www.ingramcontent.com/pod-product-compliance
Ingram Content Group UK Ltd.
Pitfield, Milton Keynes, MK11 3LW, UK
UKHW022002270726
14060UKWH00007B/741/J